COLOR TEST PAGE

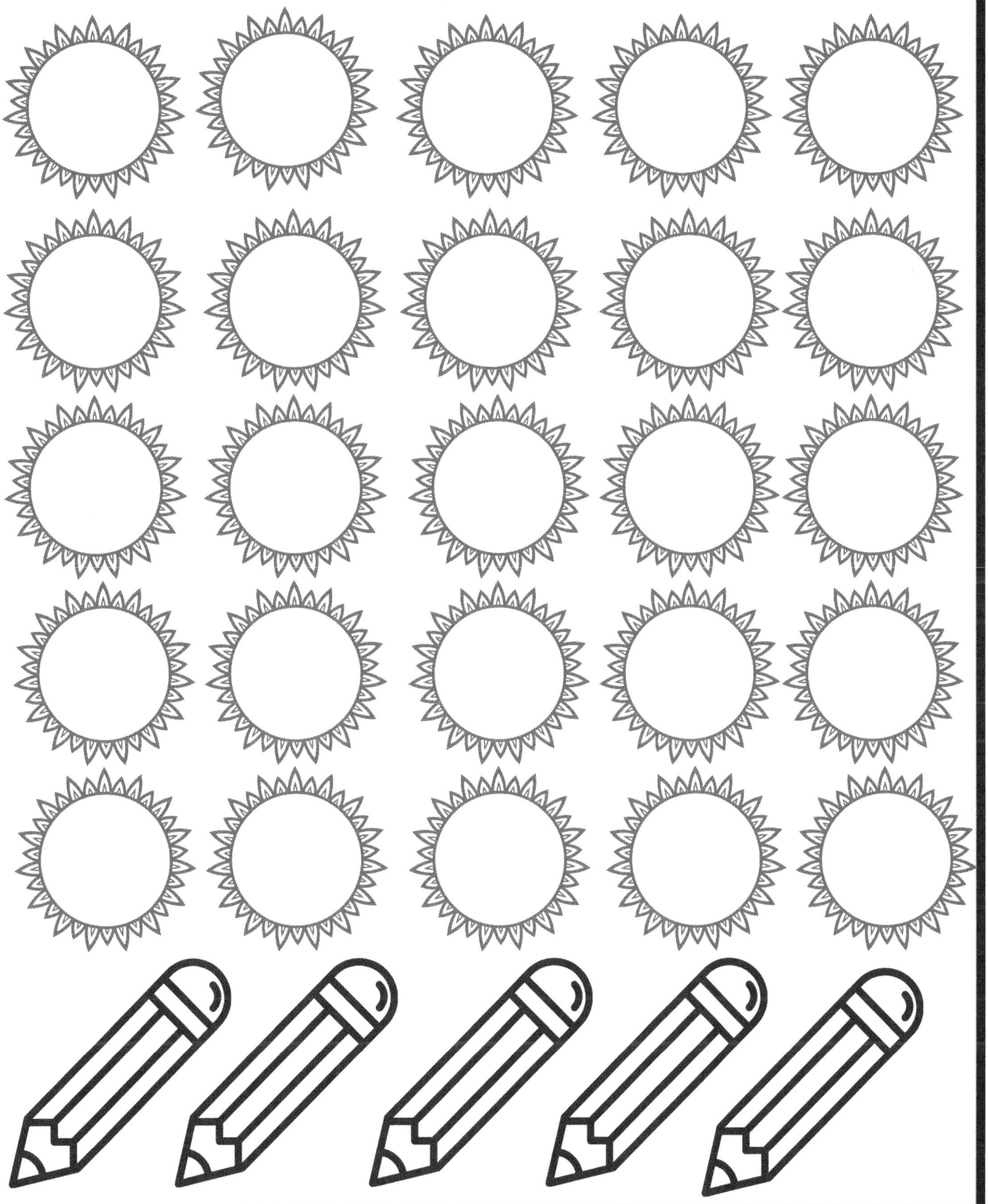

THIS BOOK BELONGS TO

HAPPY HALLOWEEN COLORING BOOK AGES 3-7

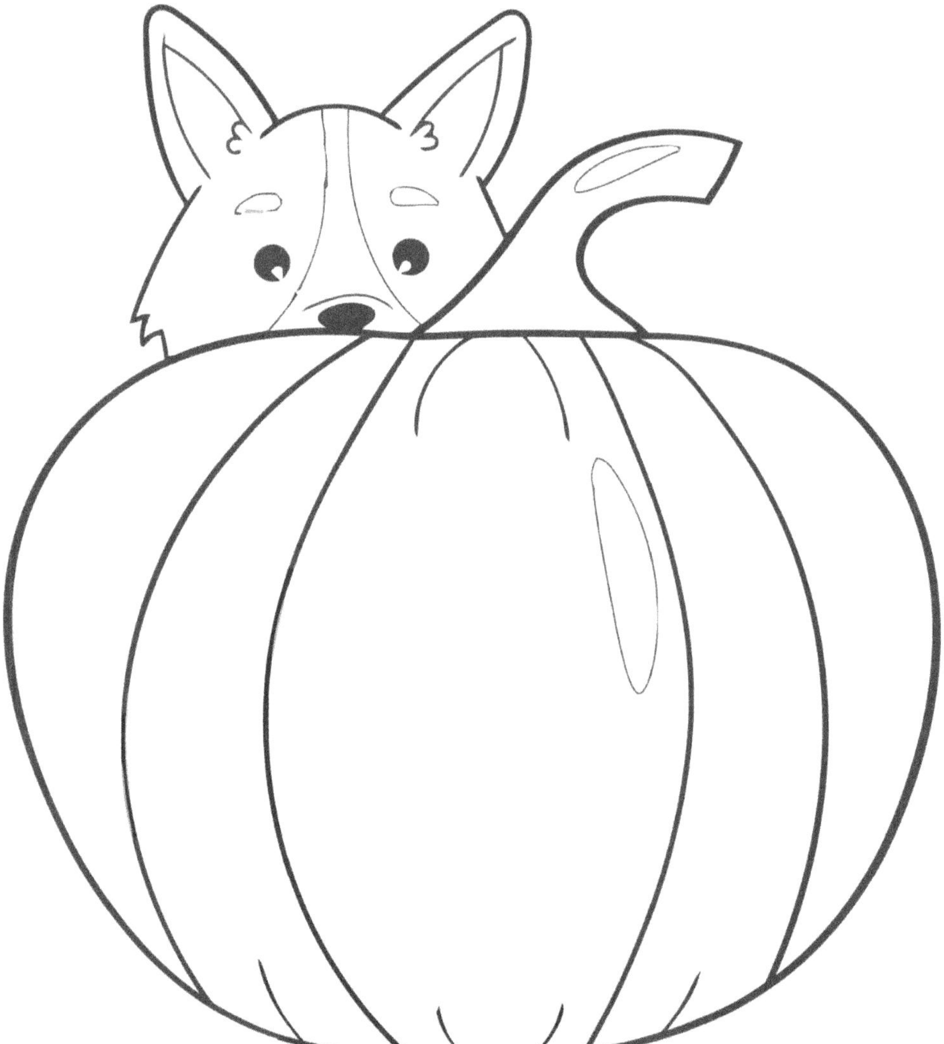

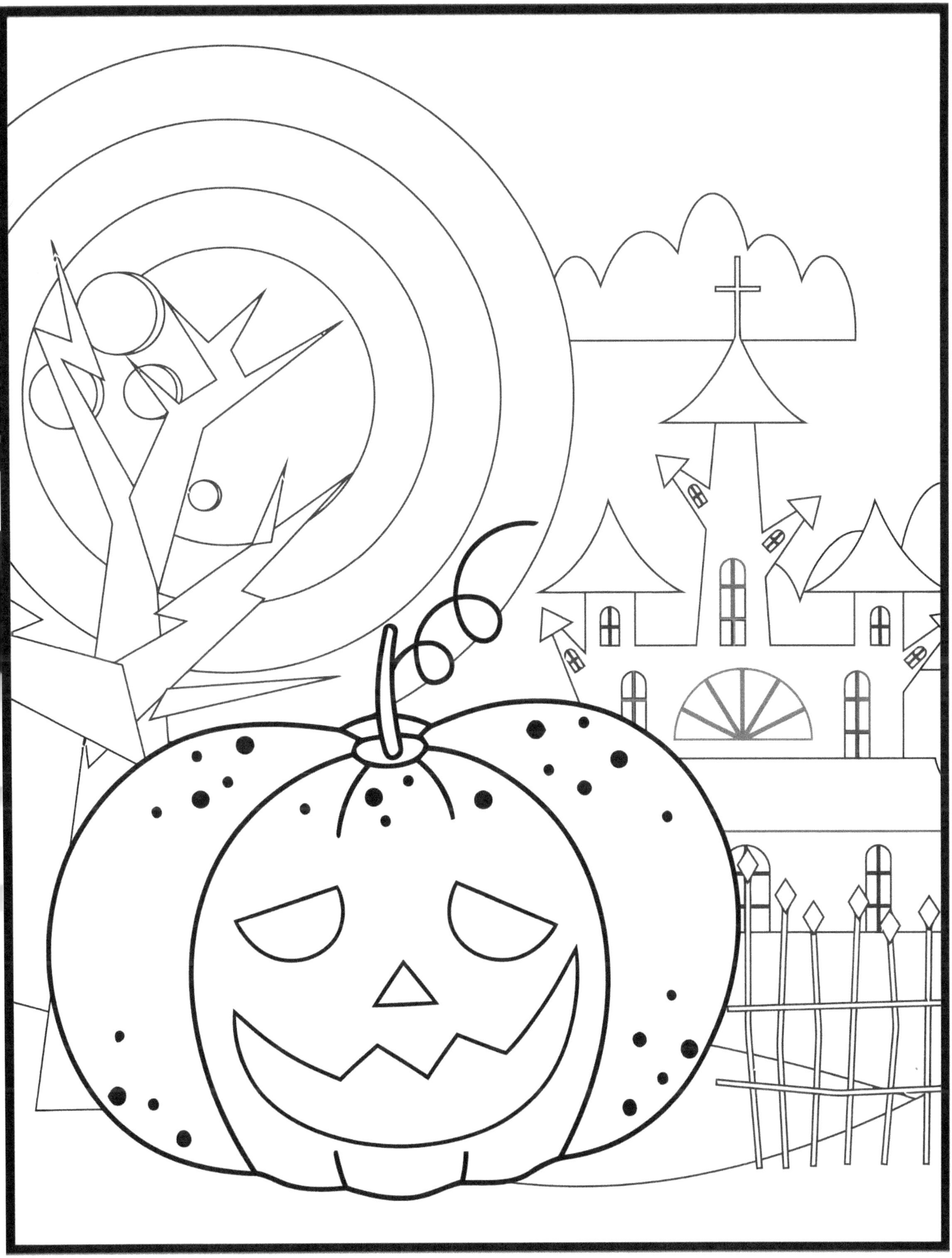

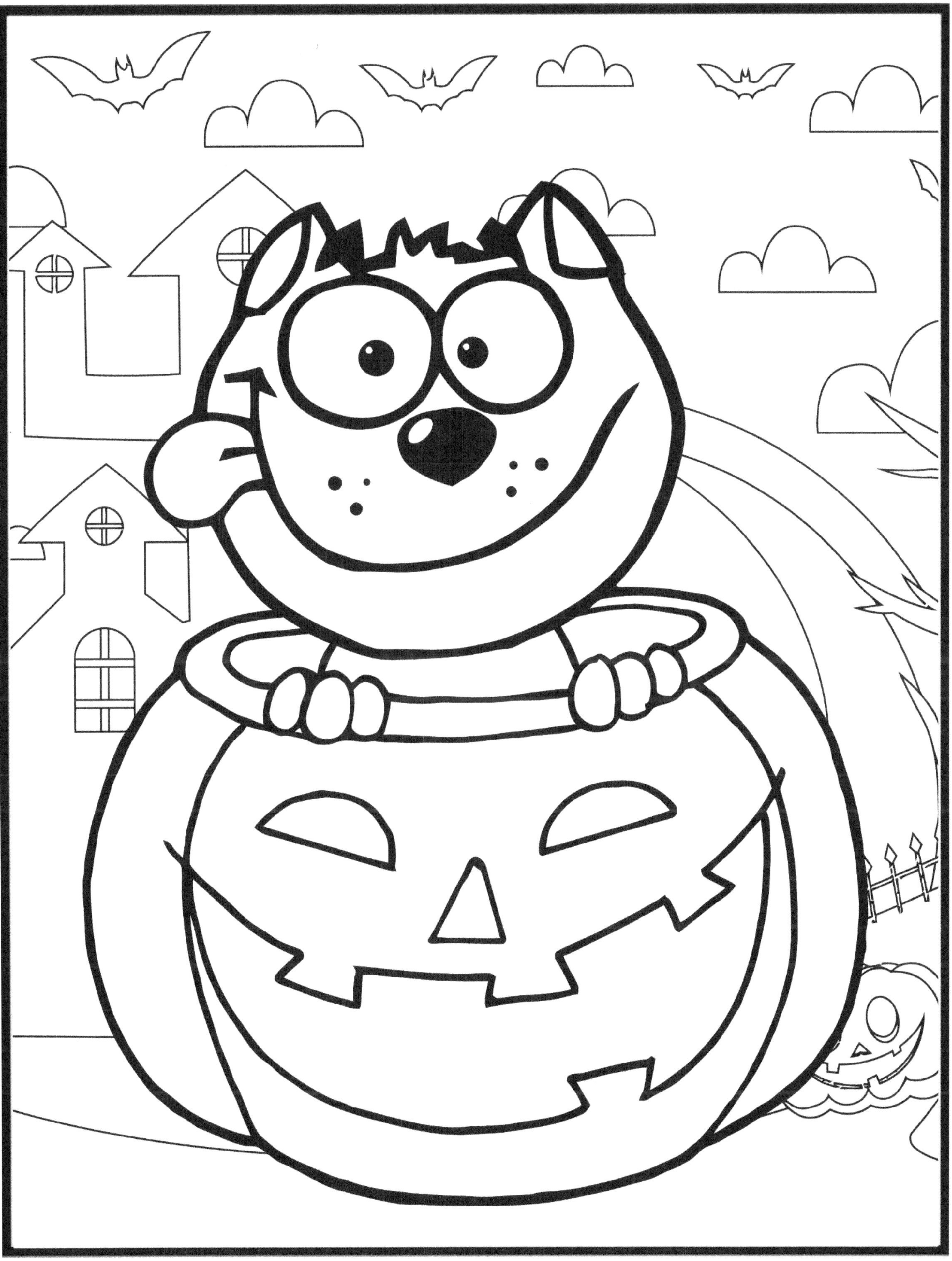

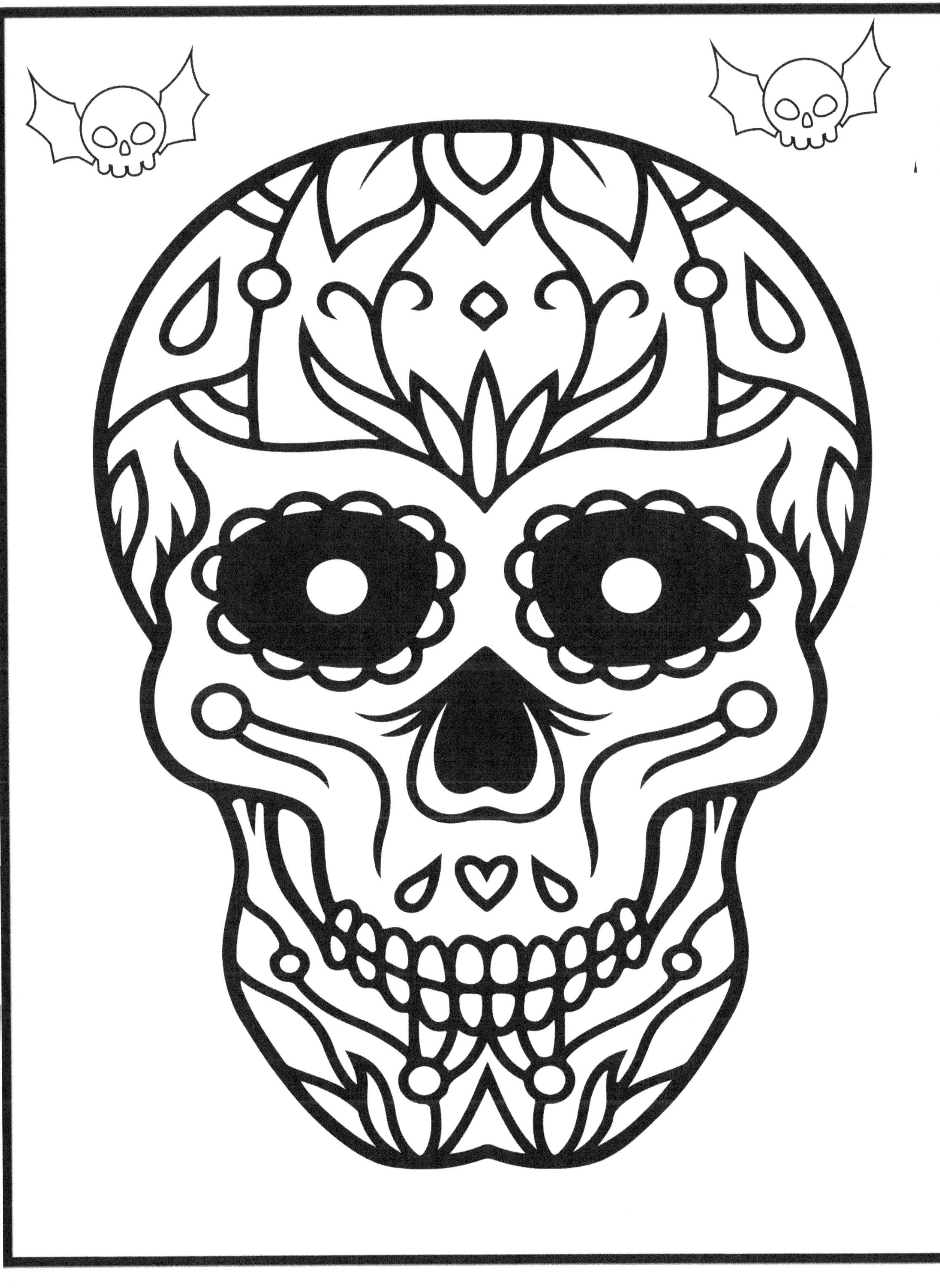

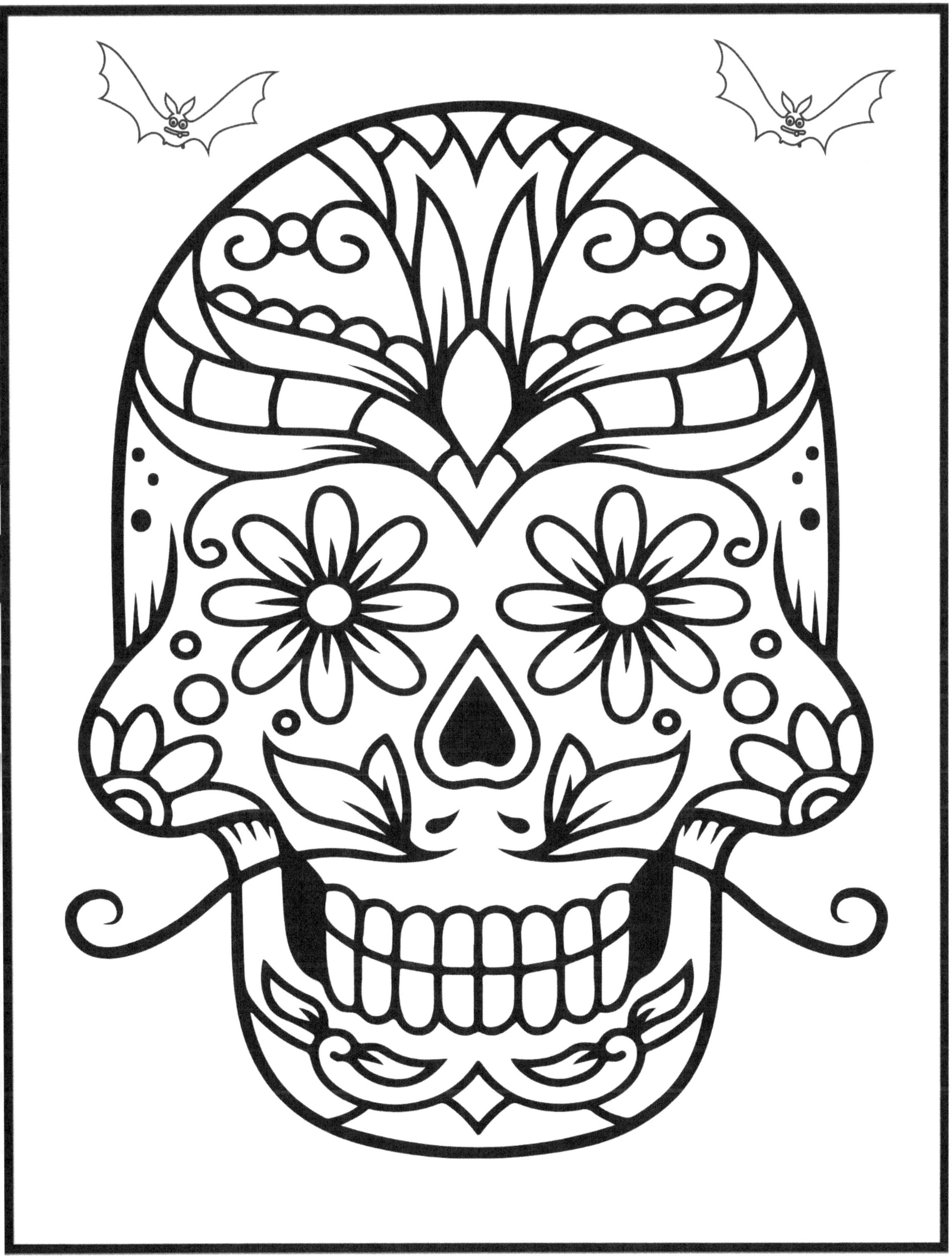

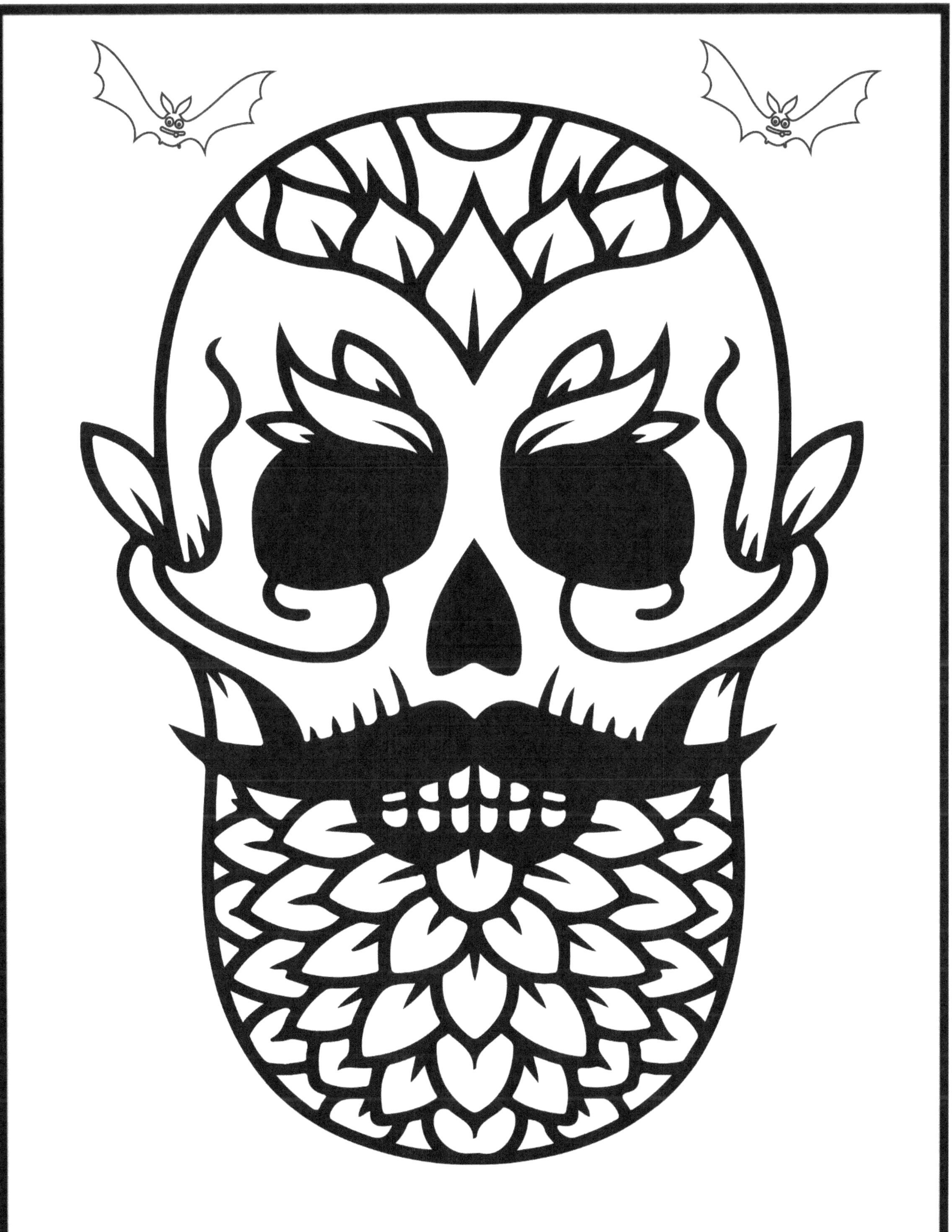

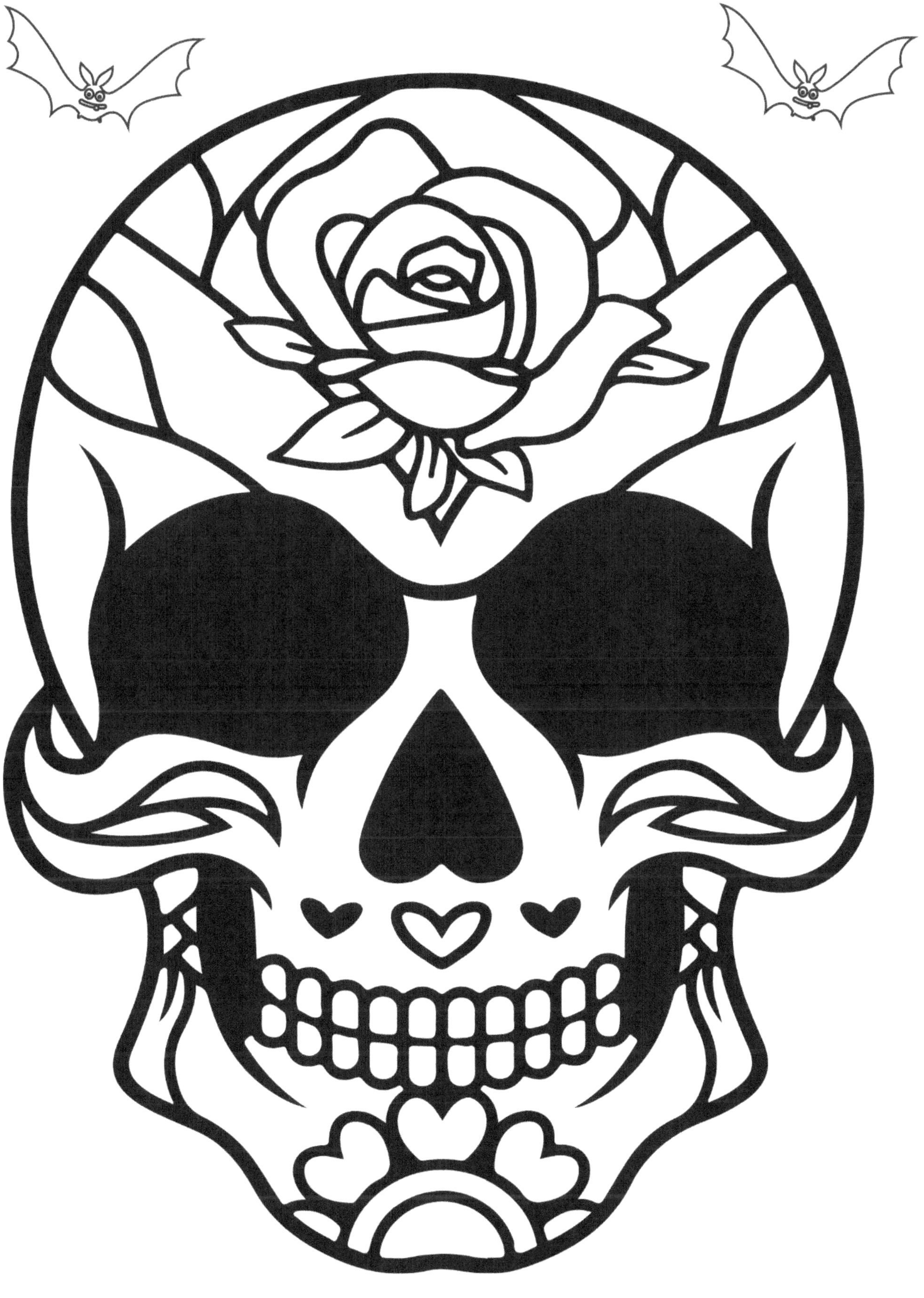

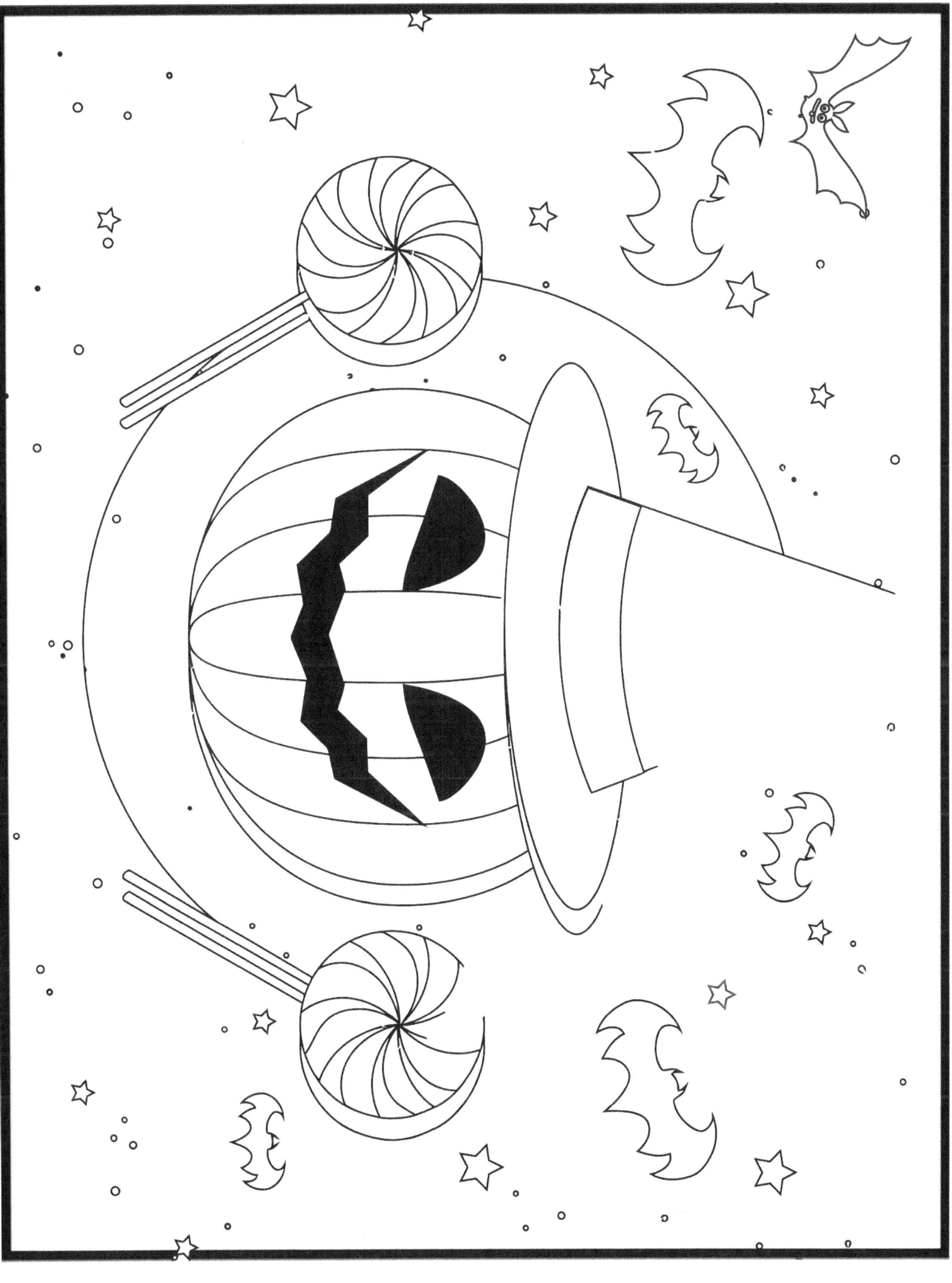

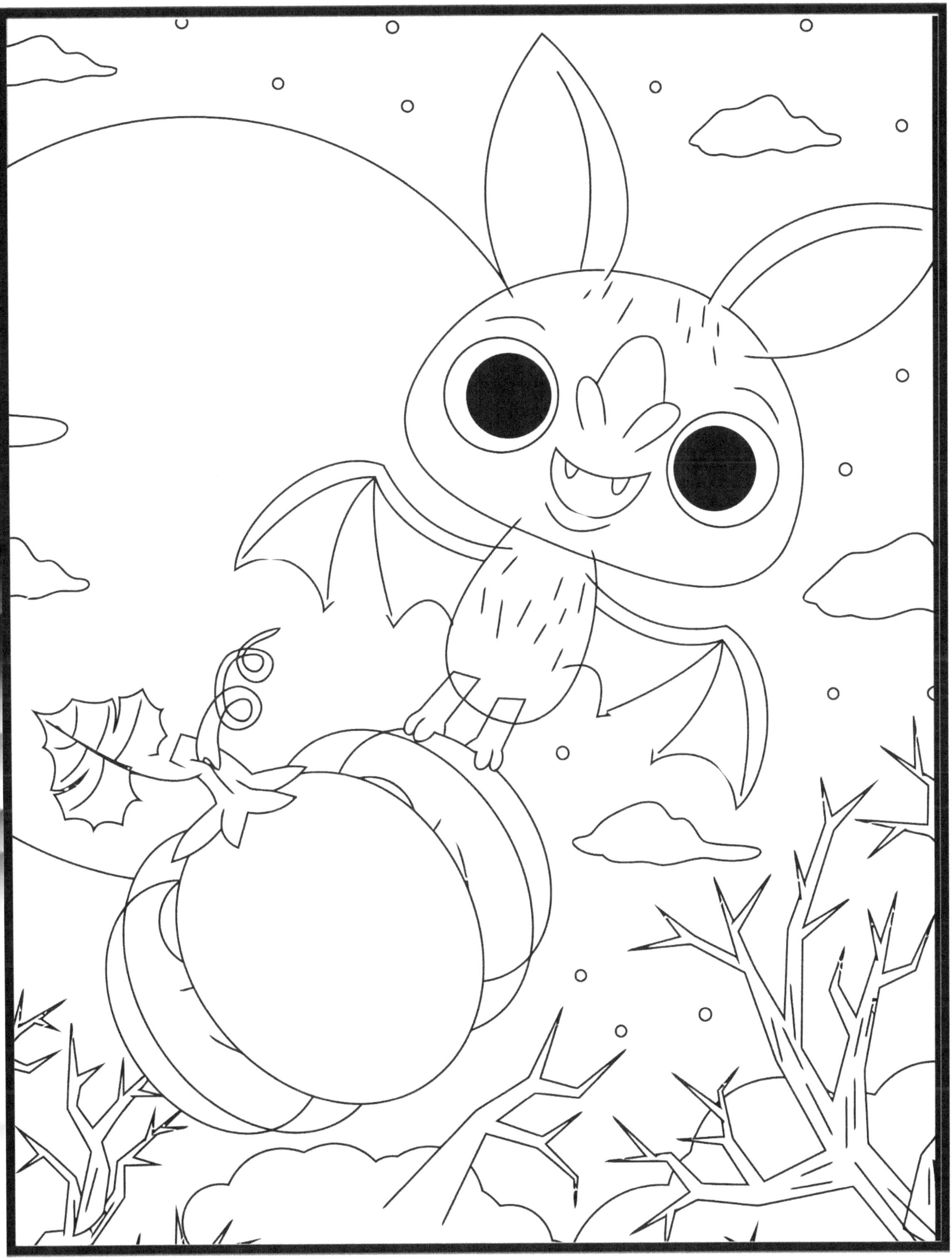

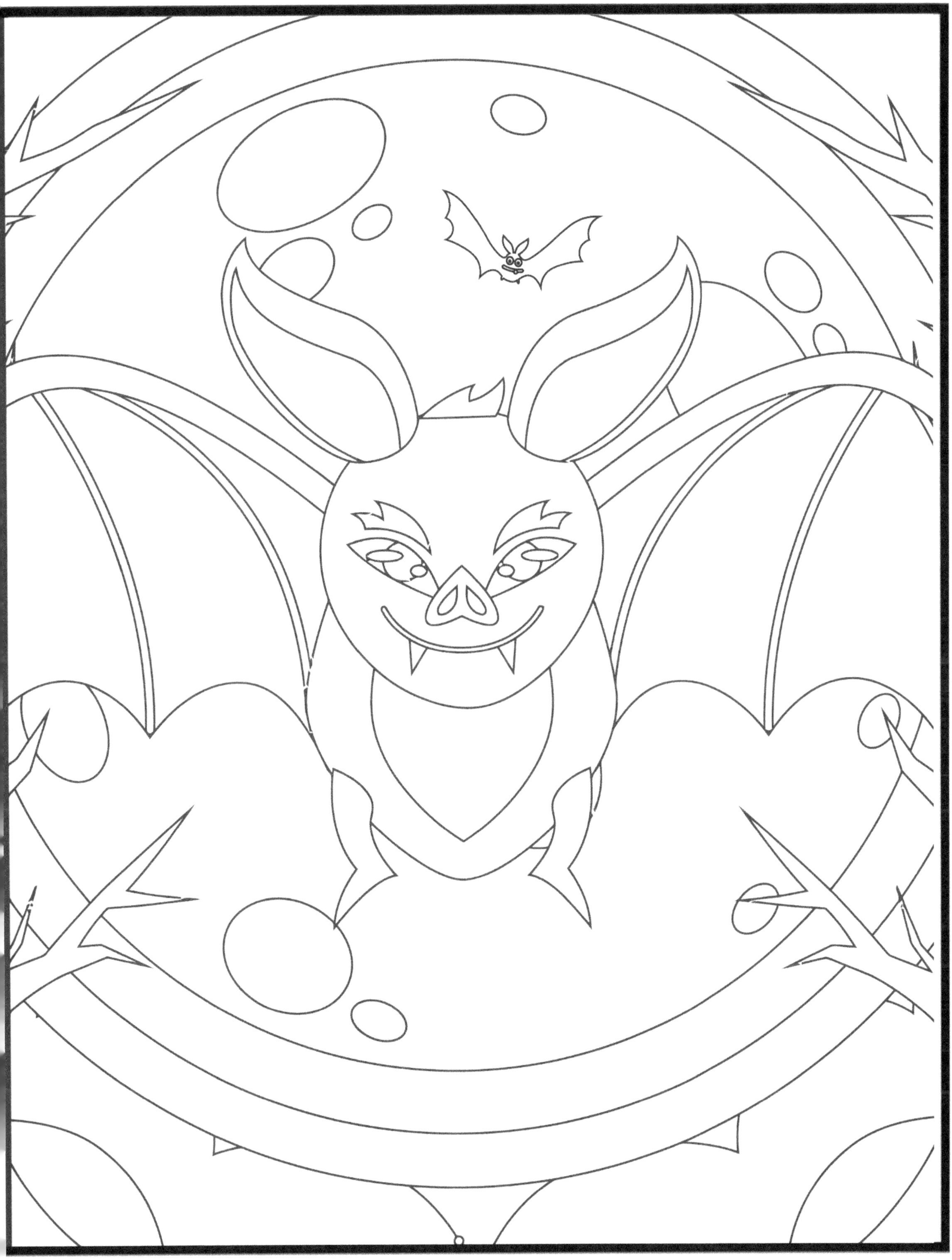

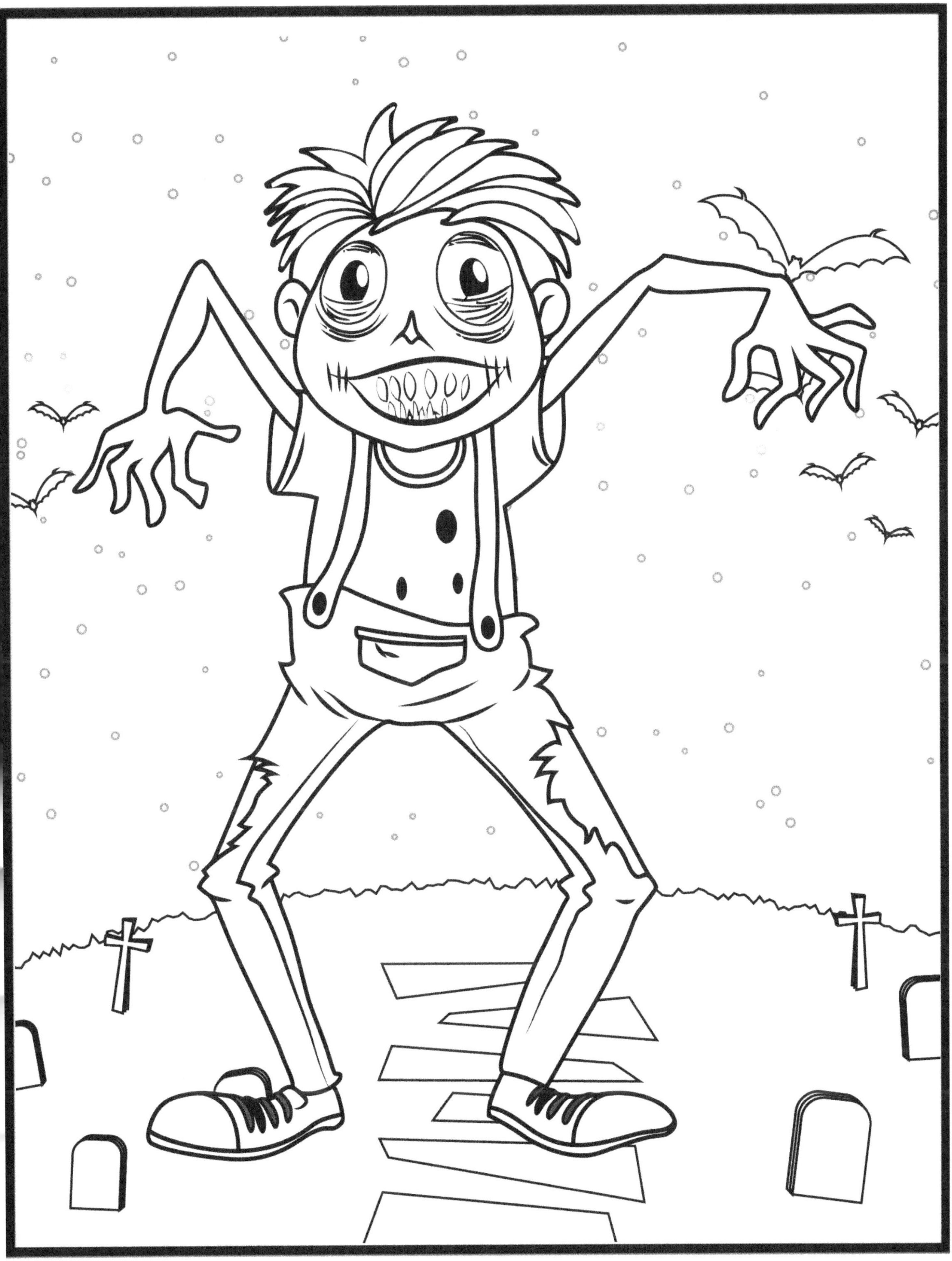

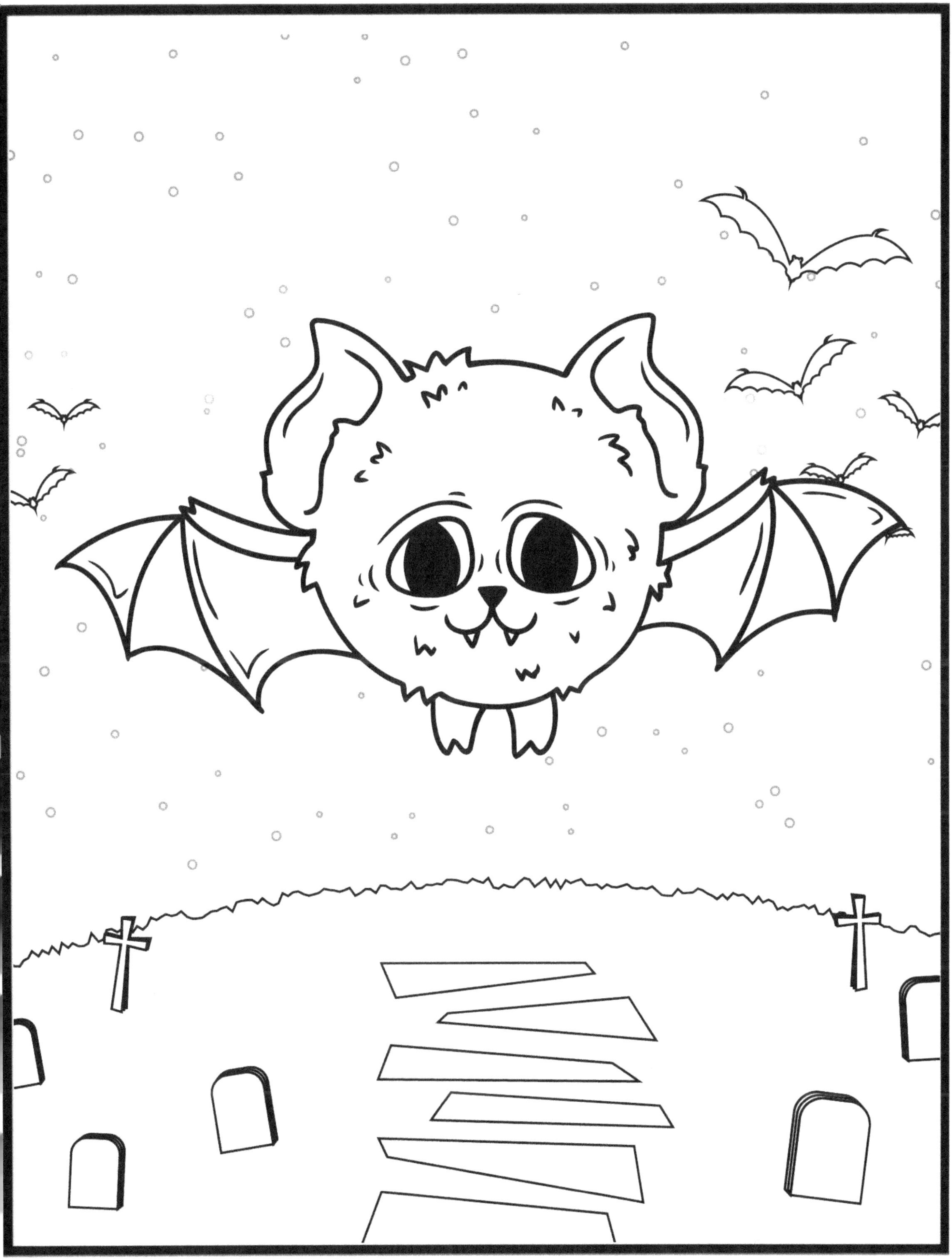

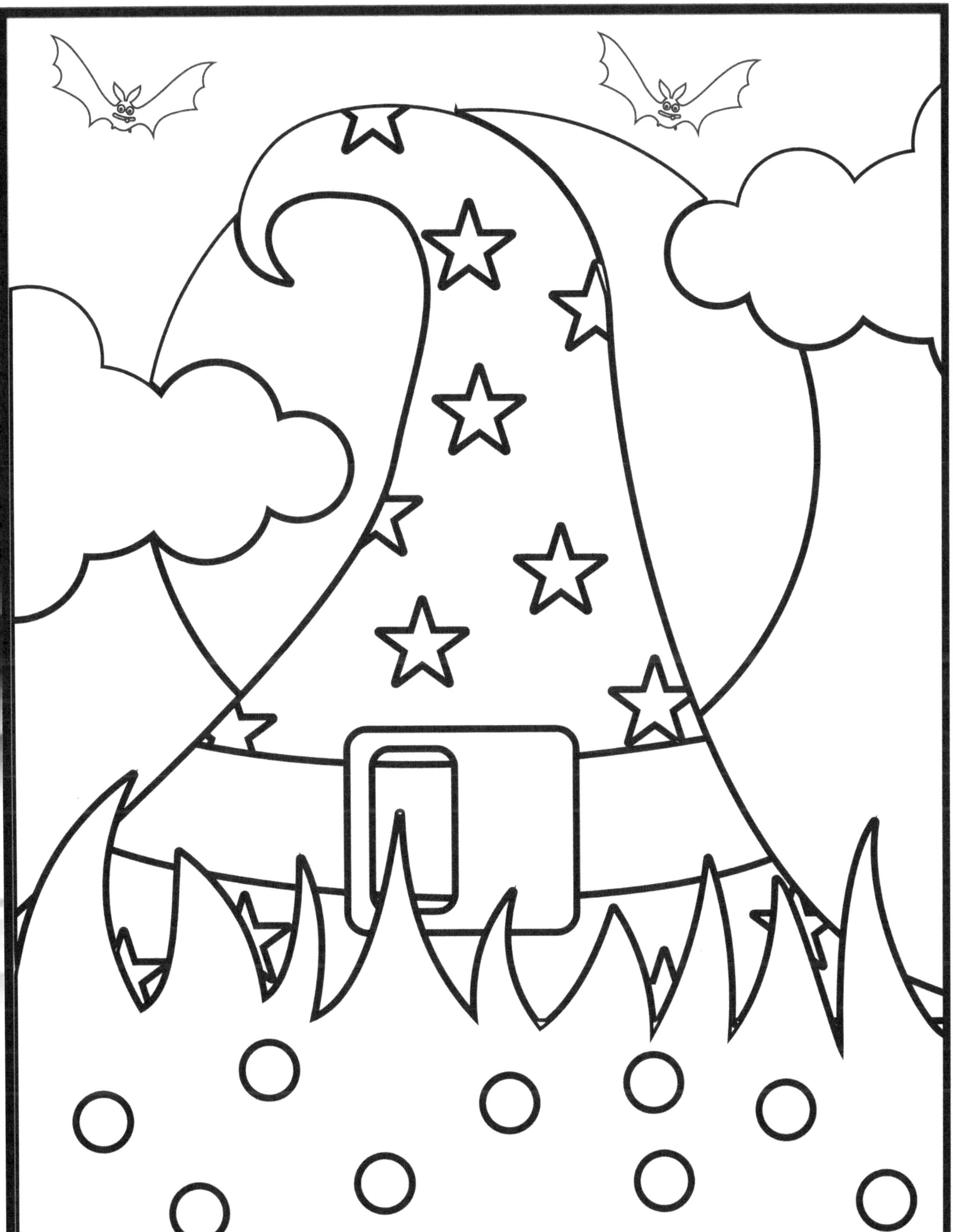

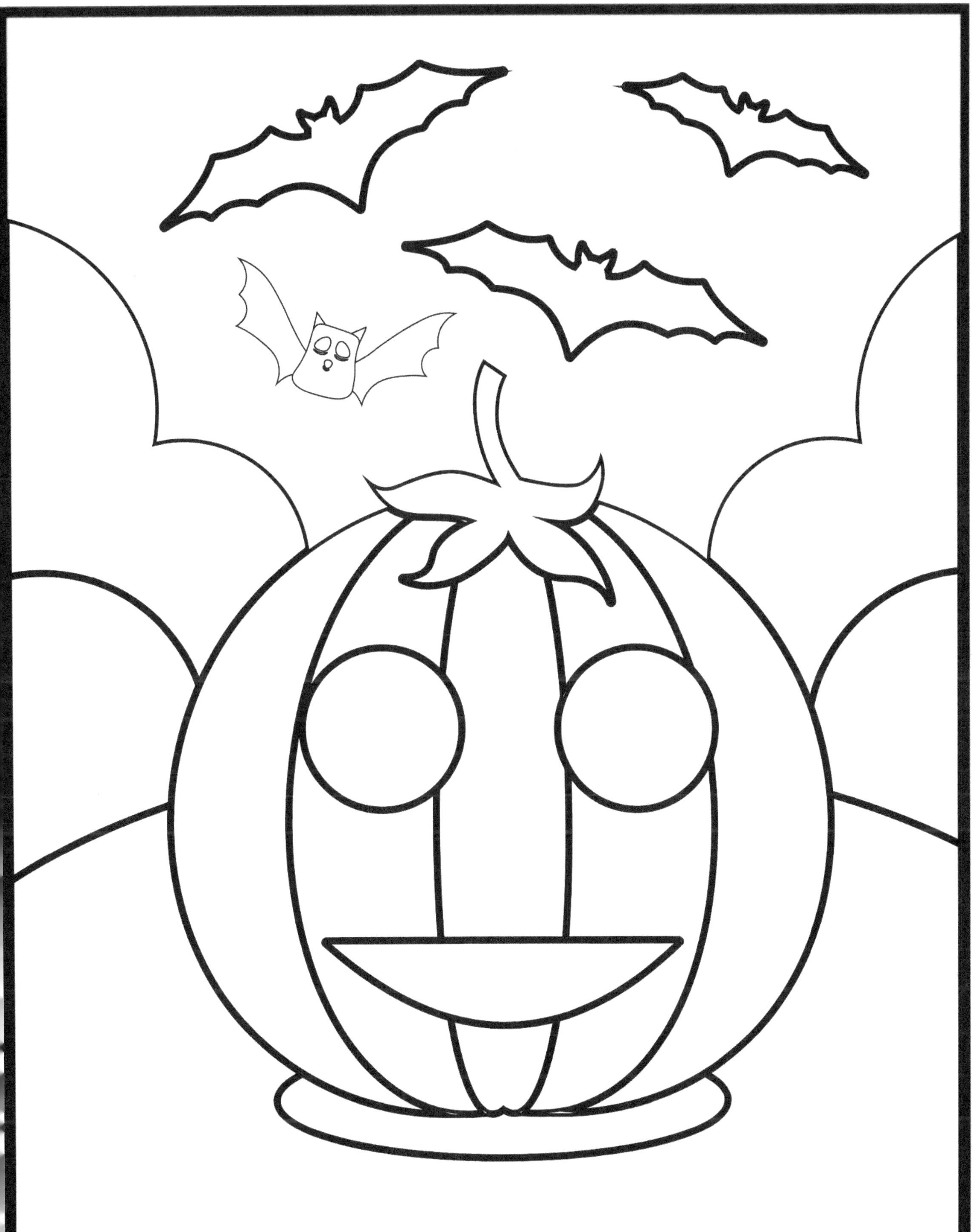

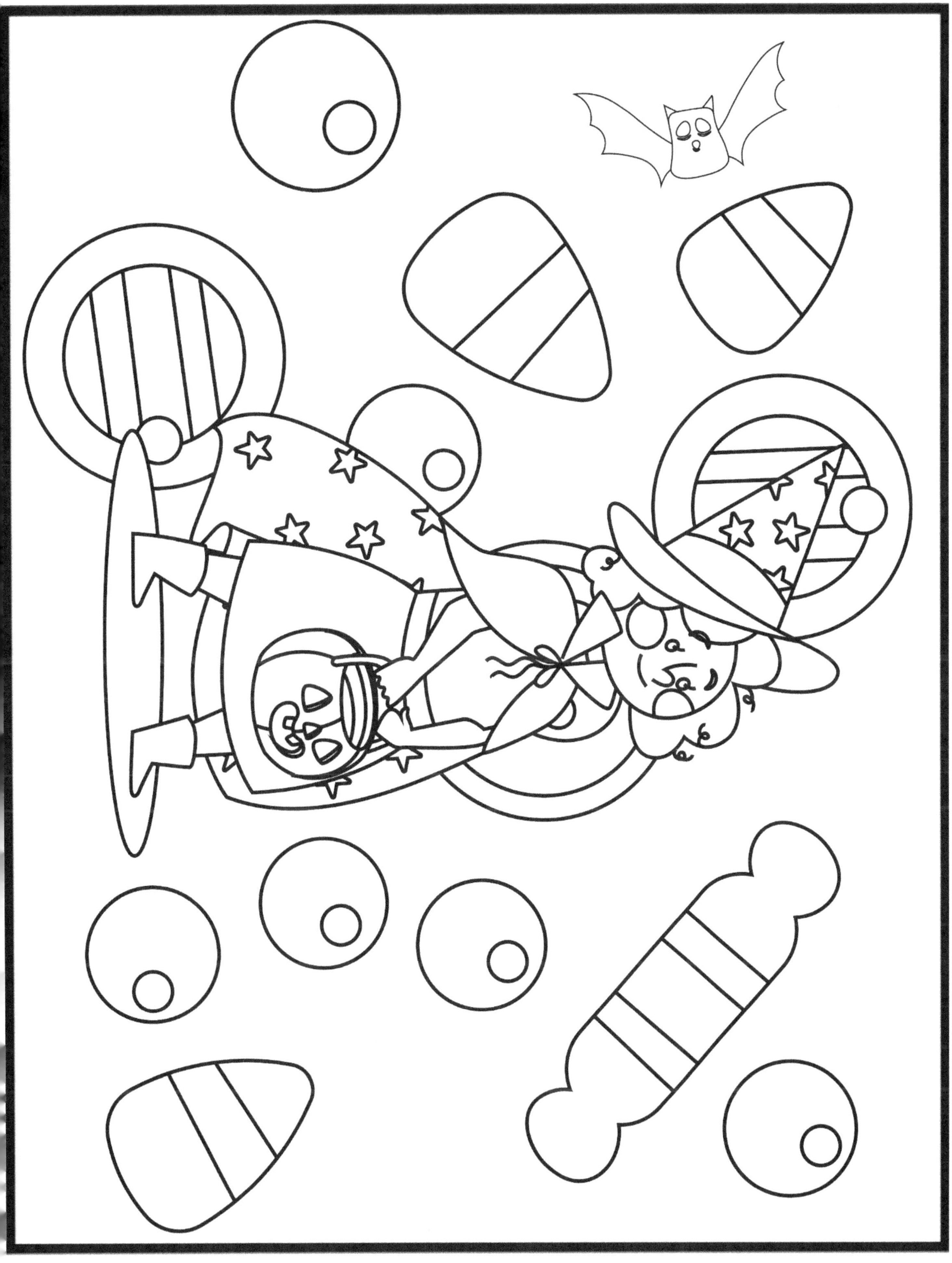

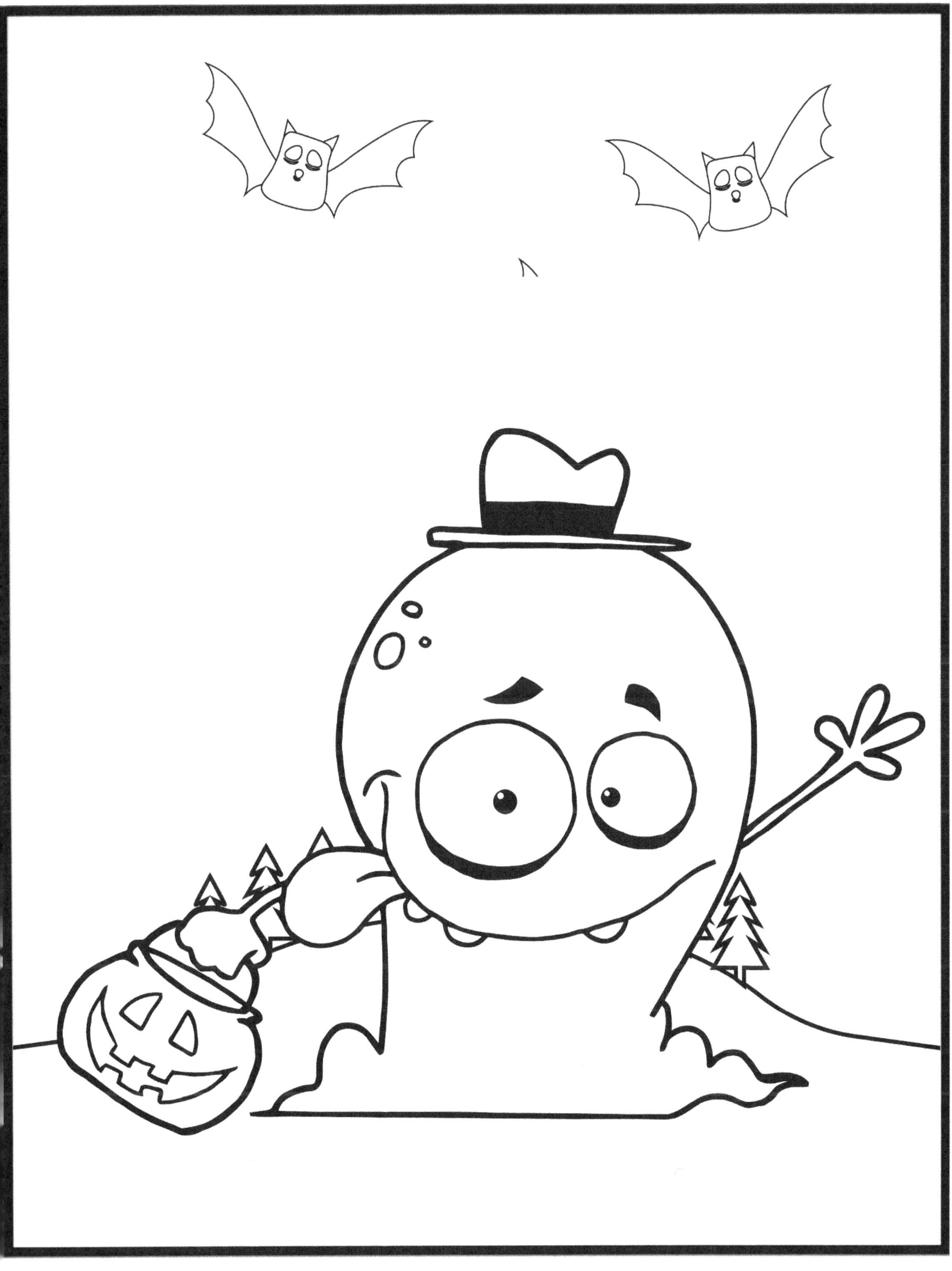

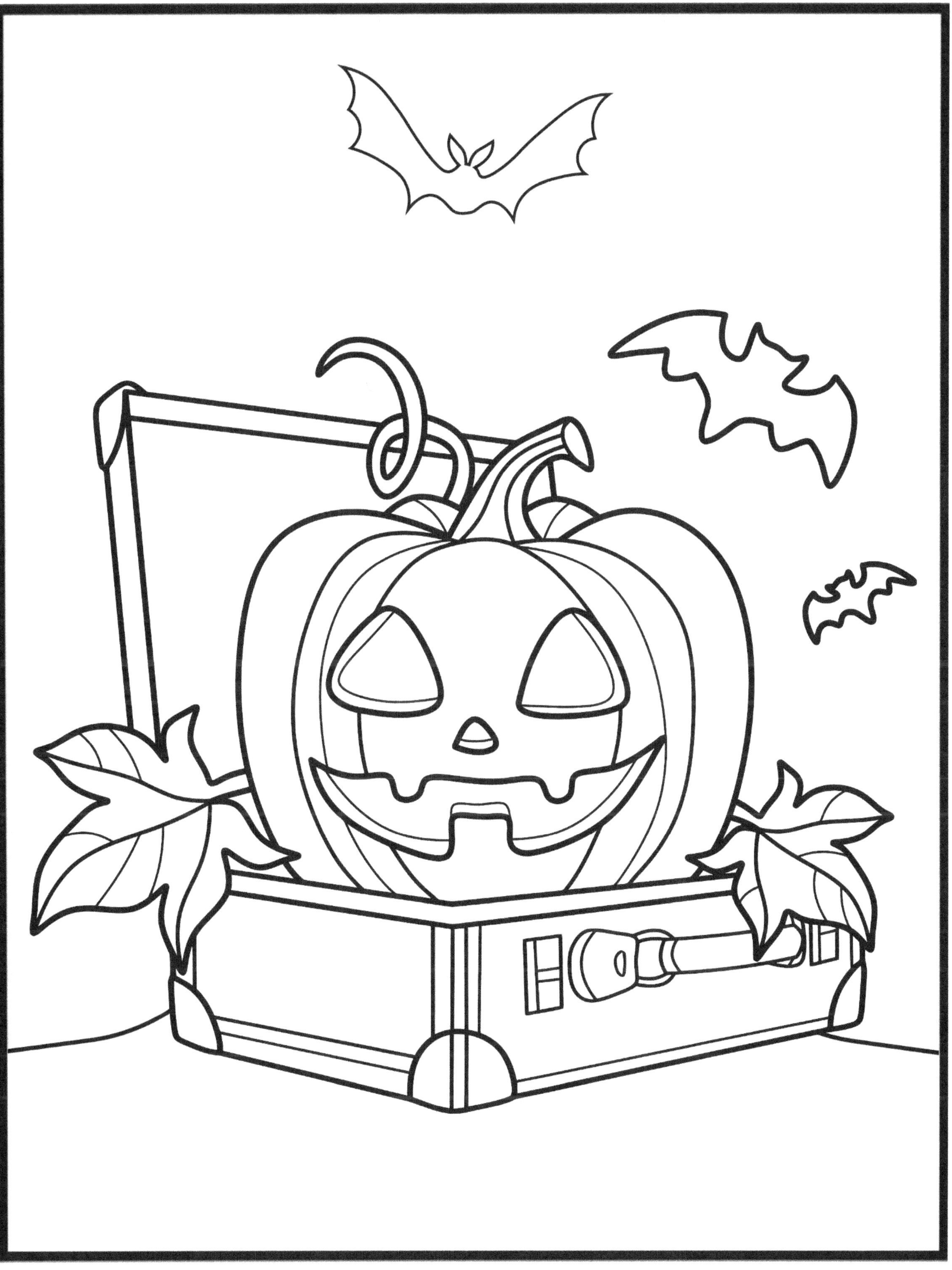

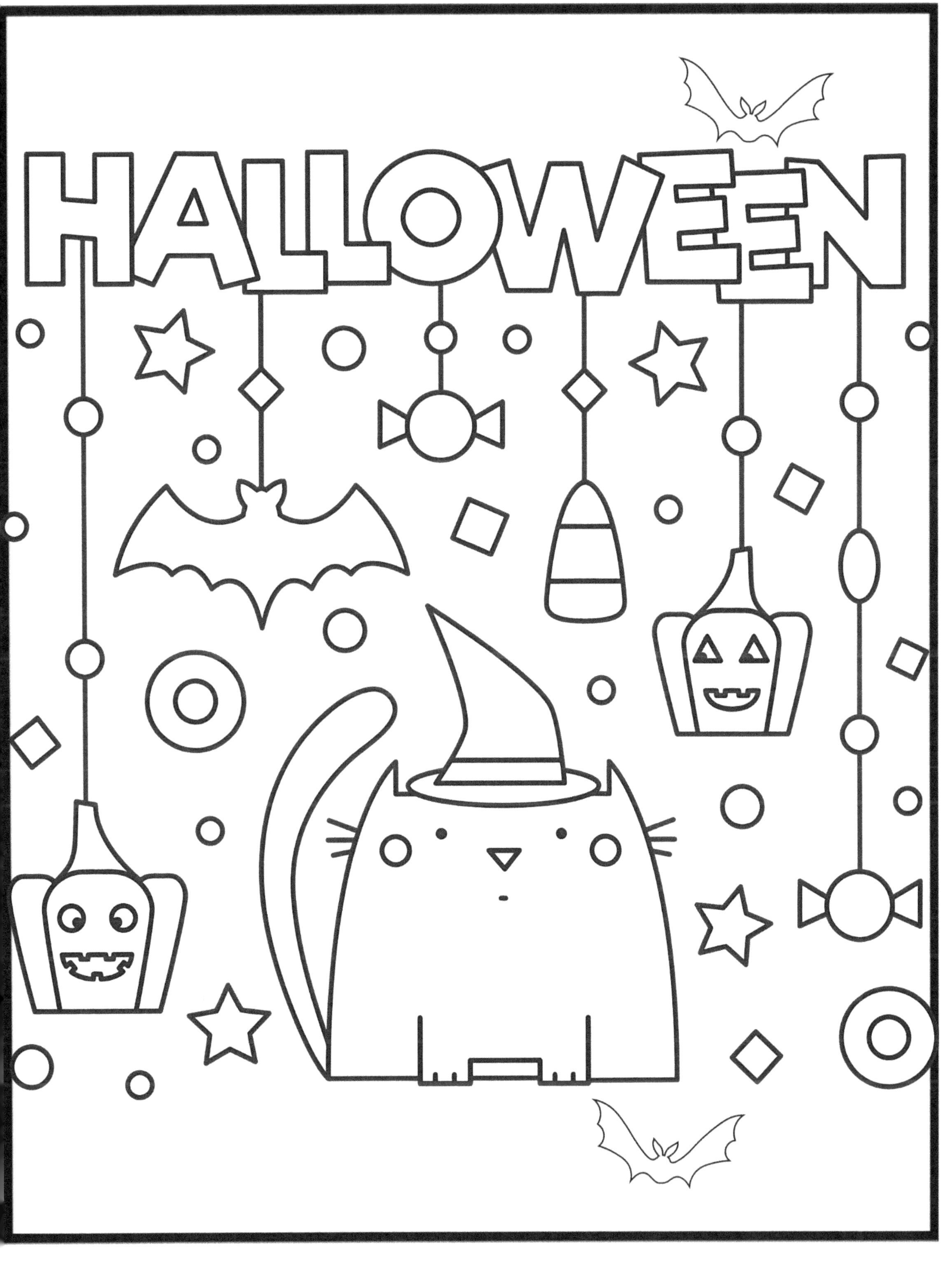
HALLOWEEN

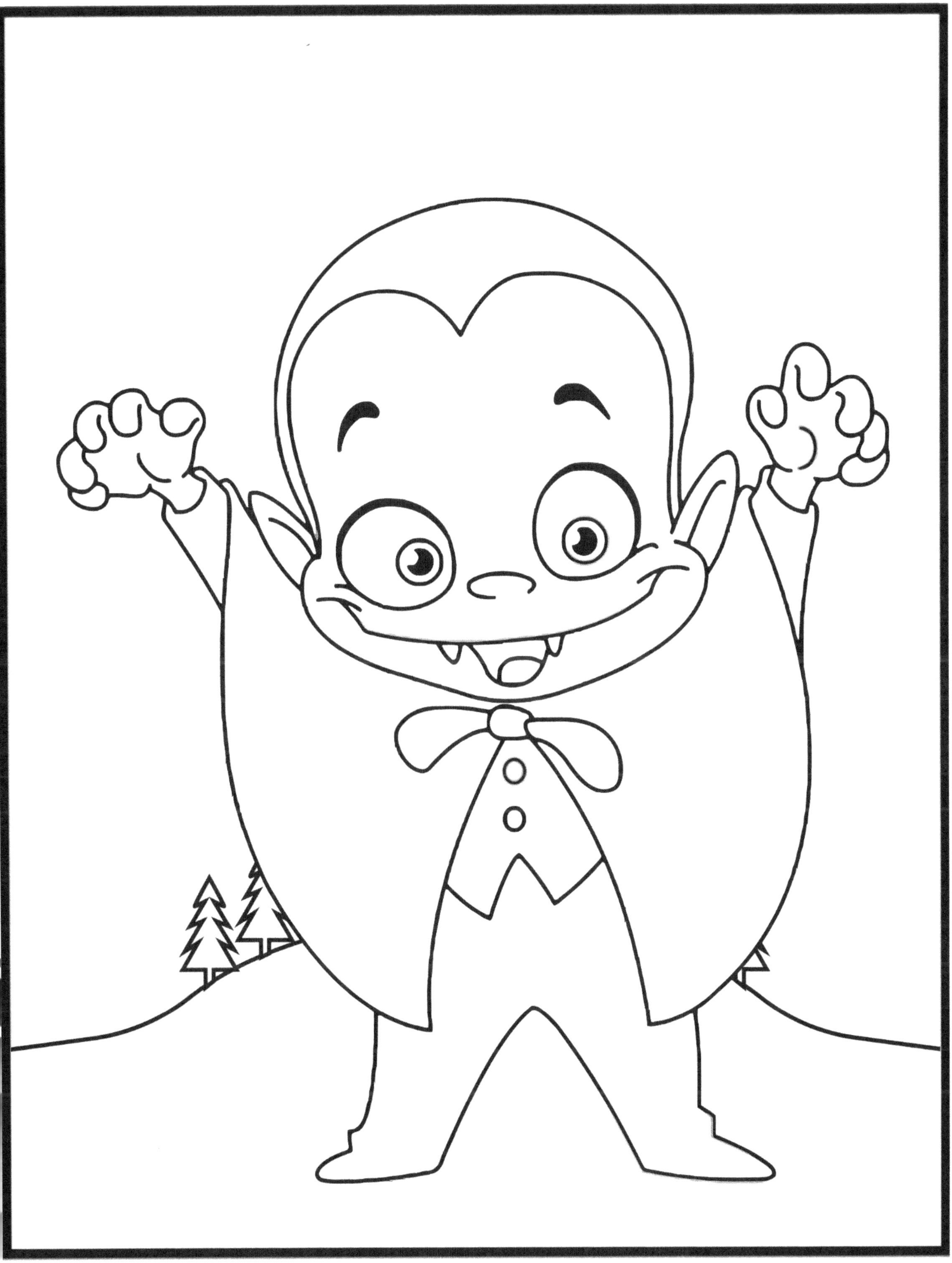

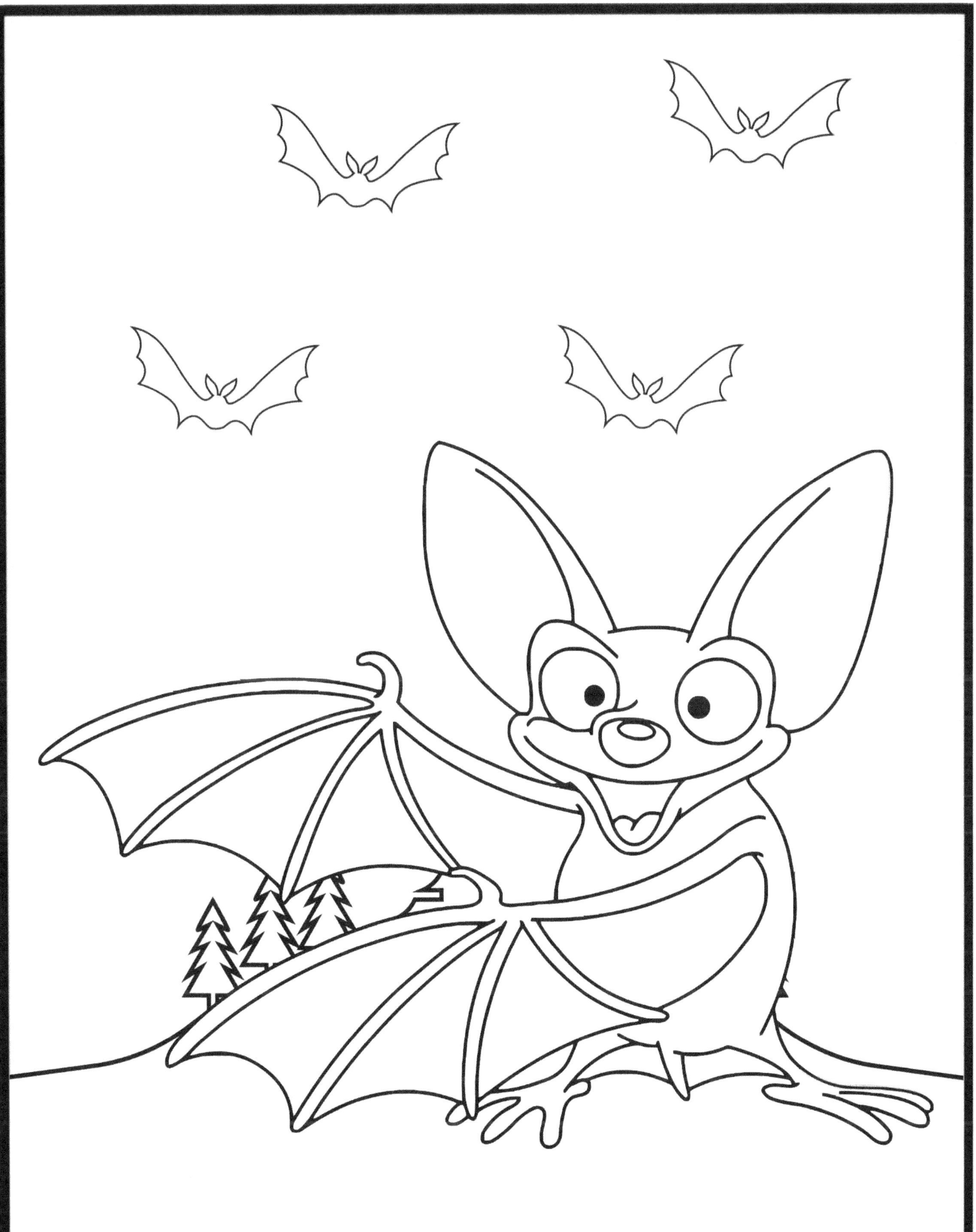

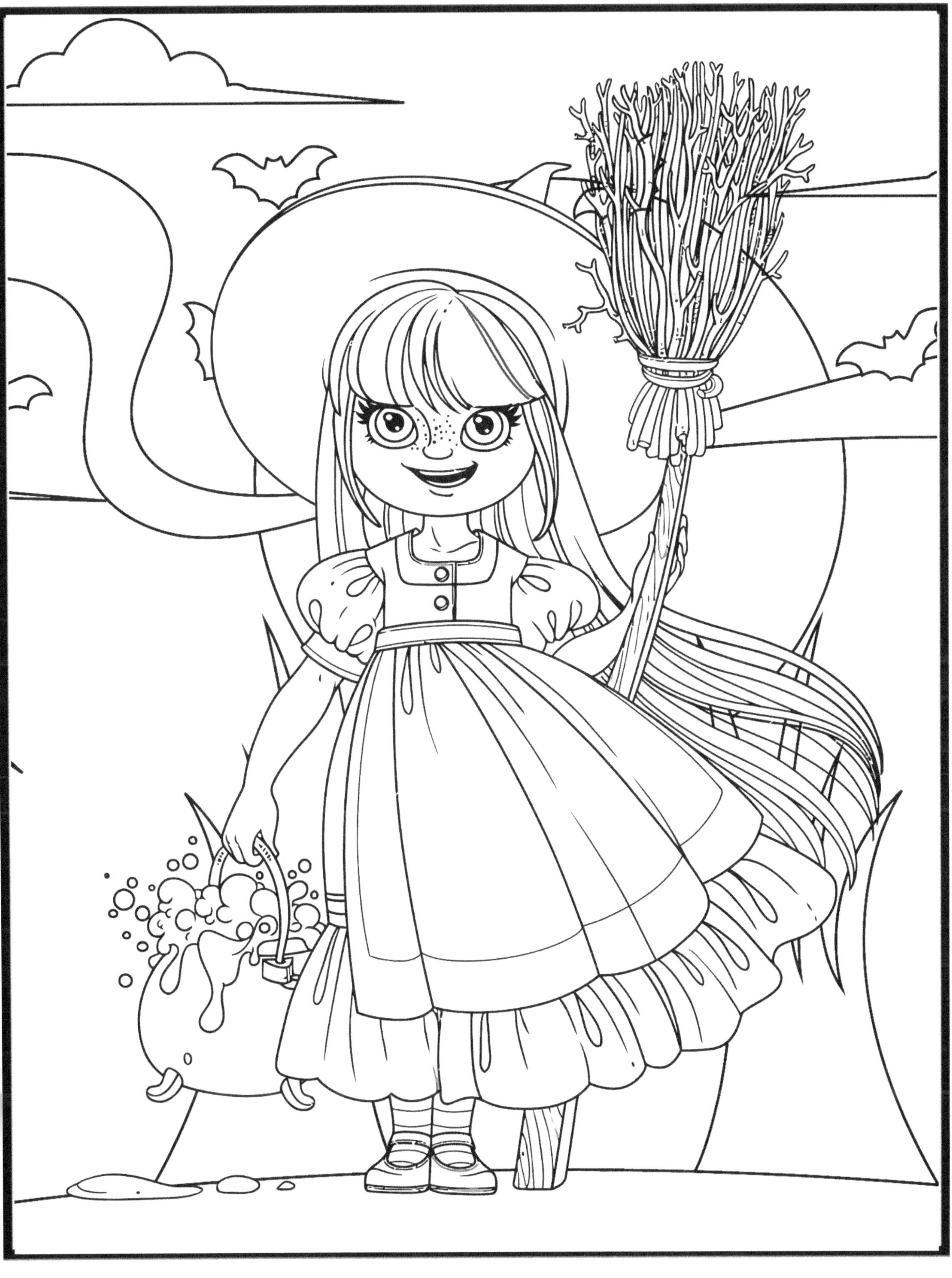

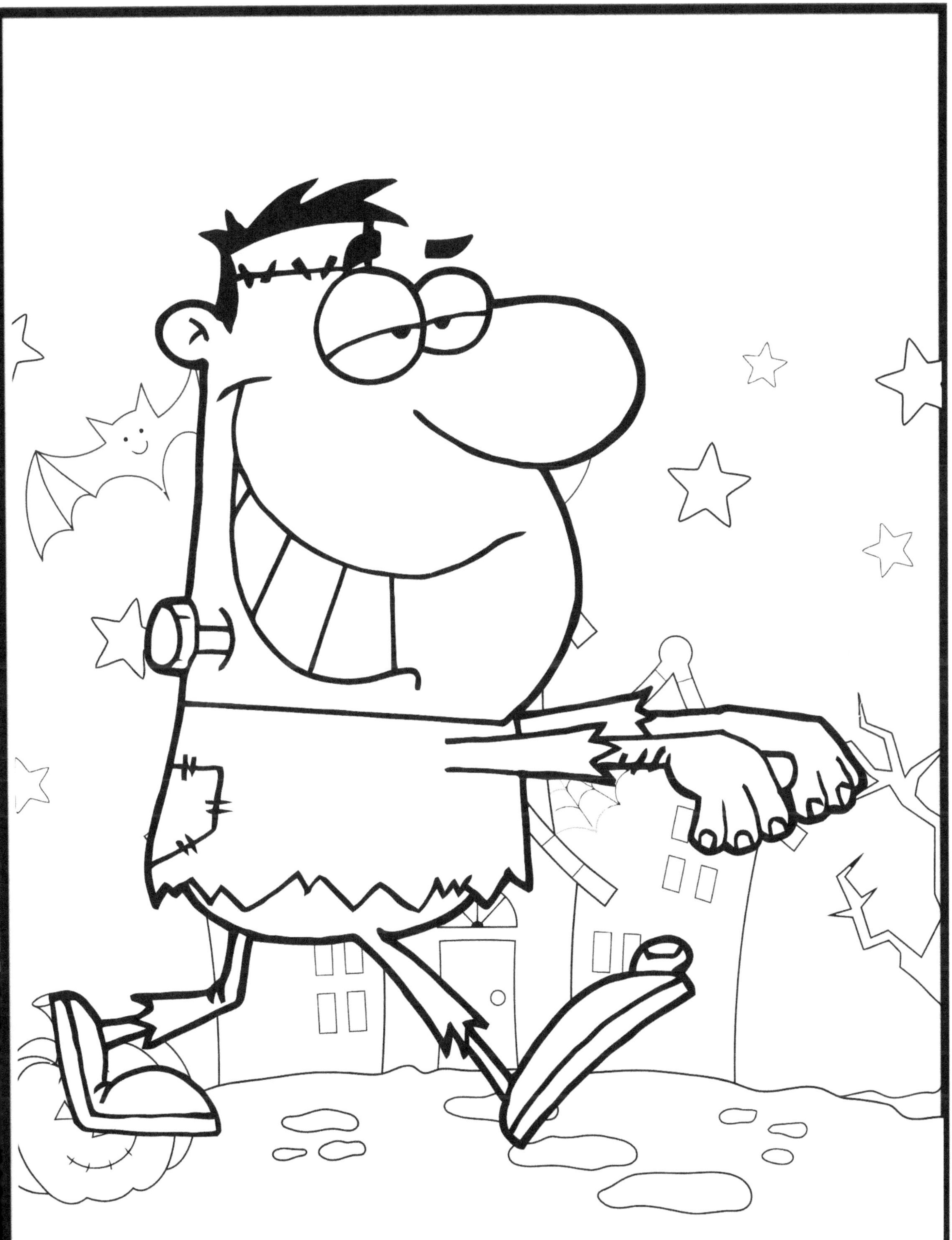

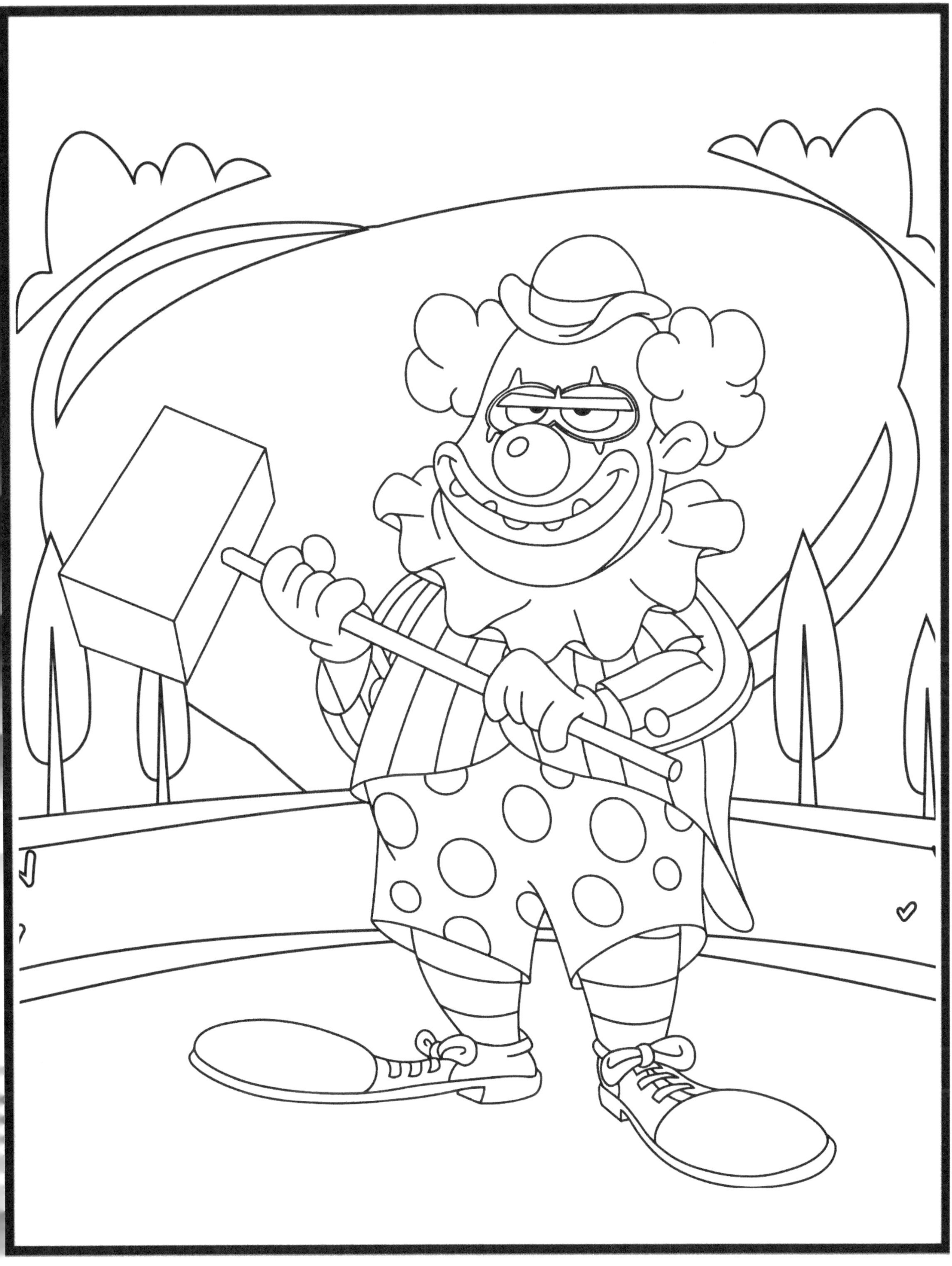

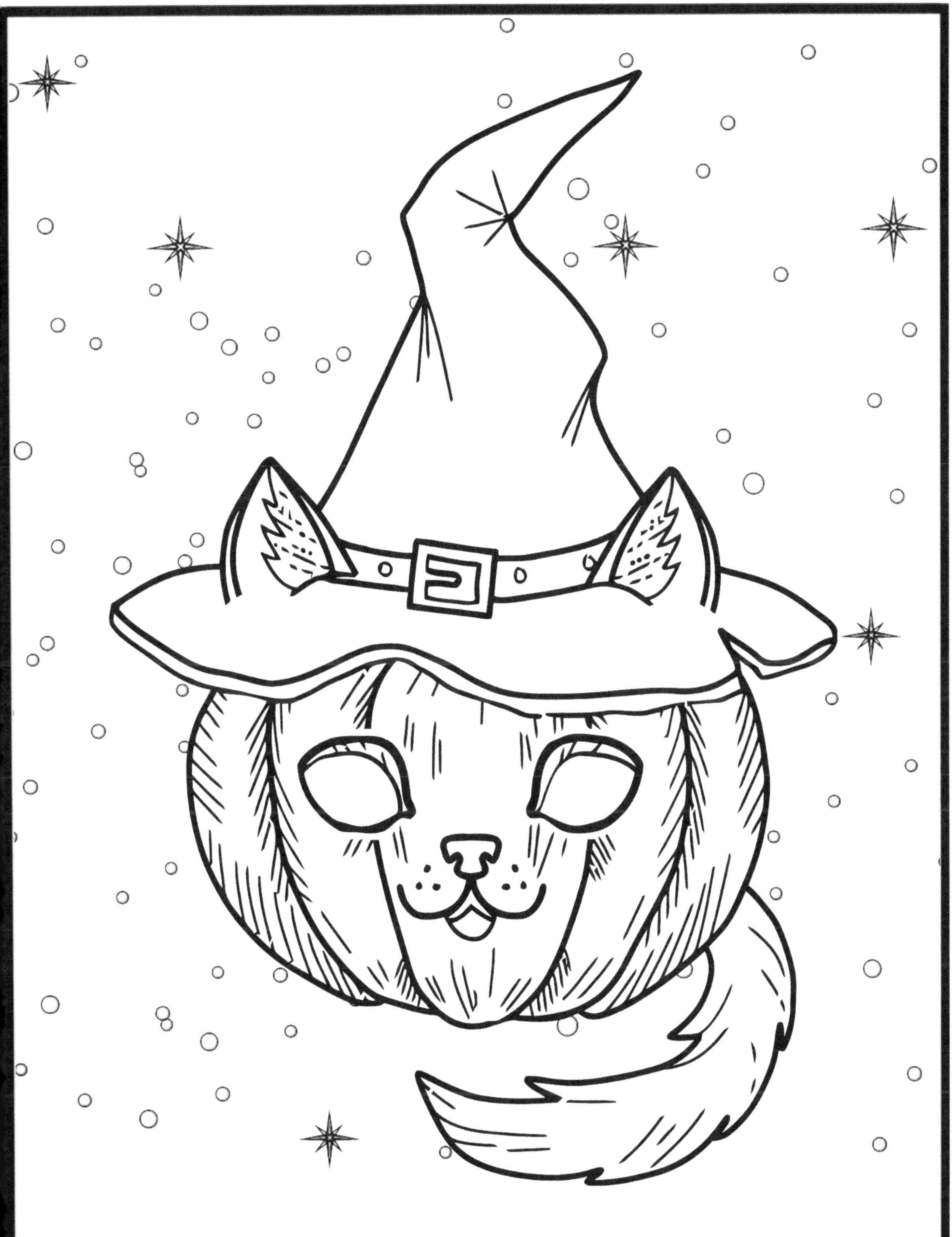

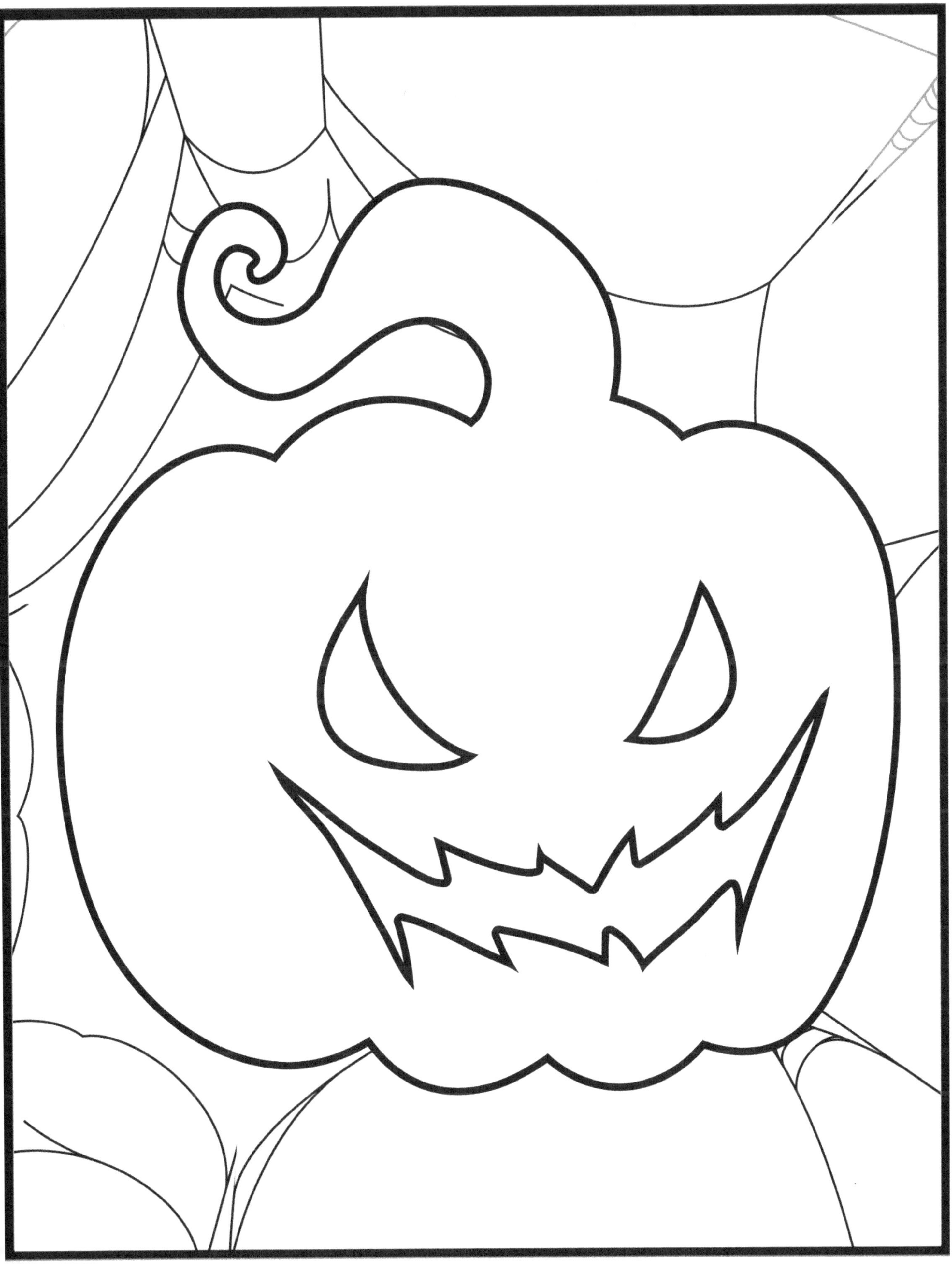

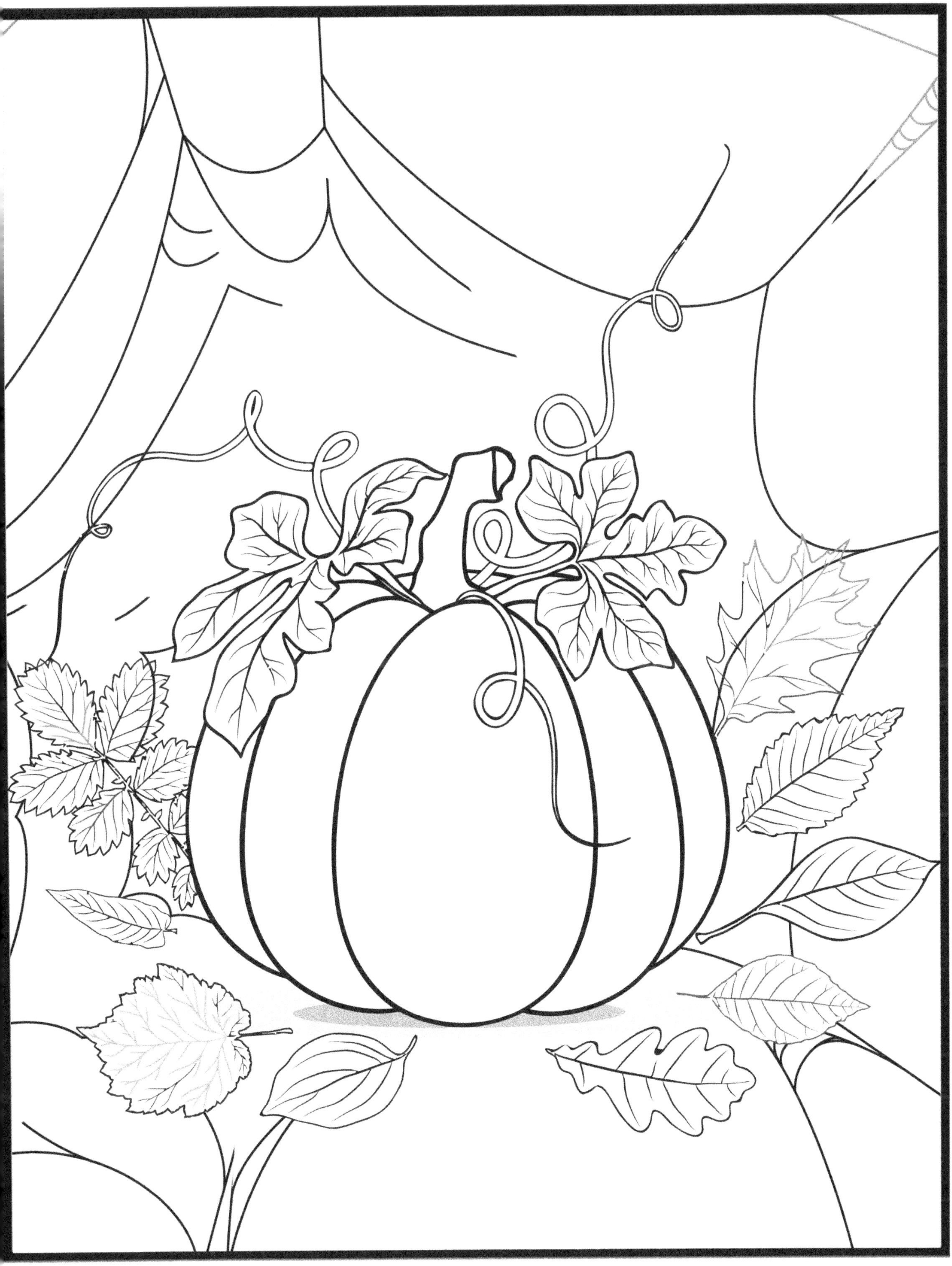

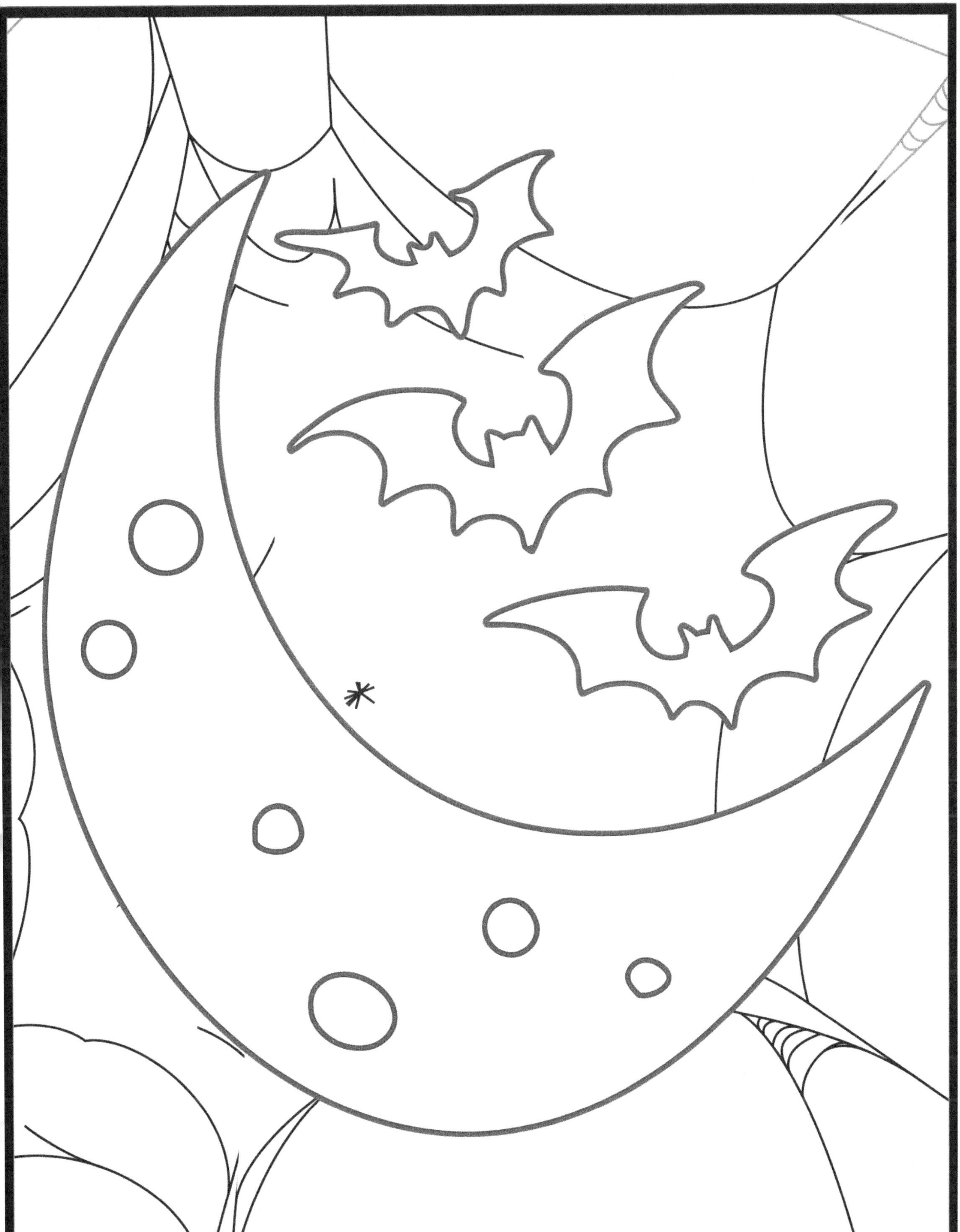

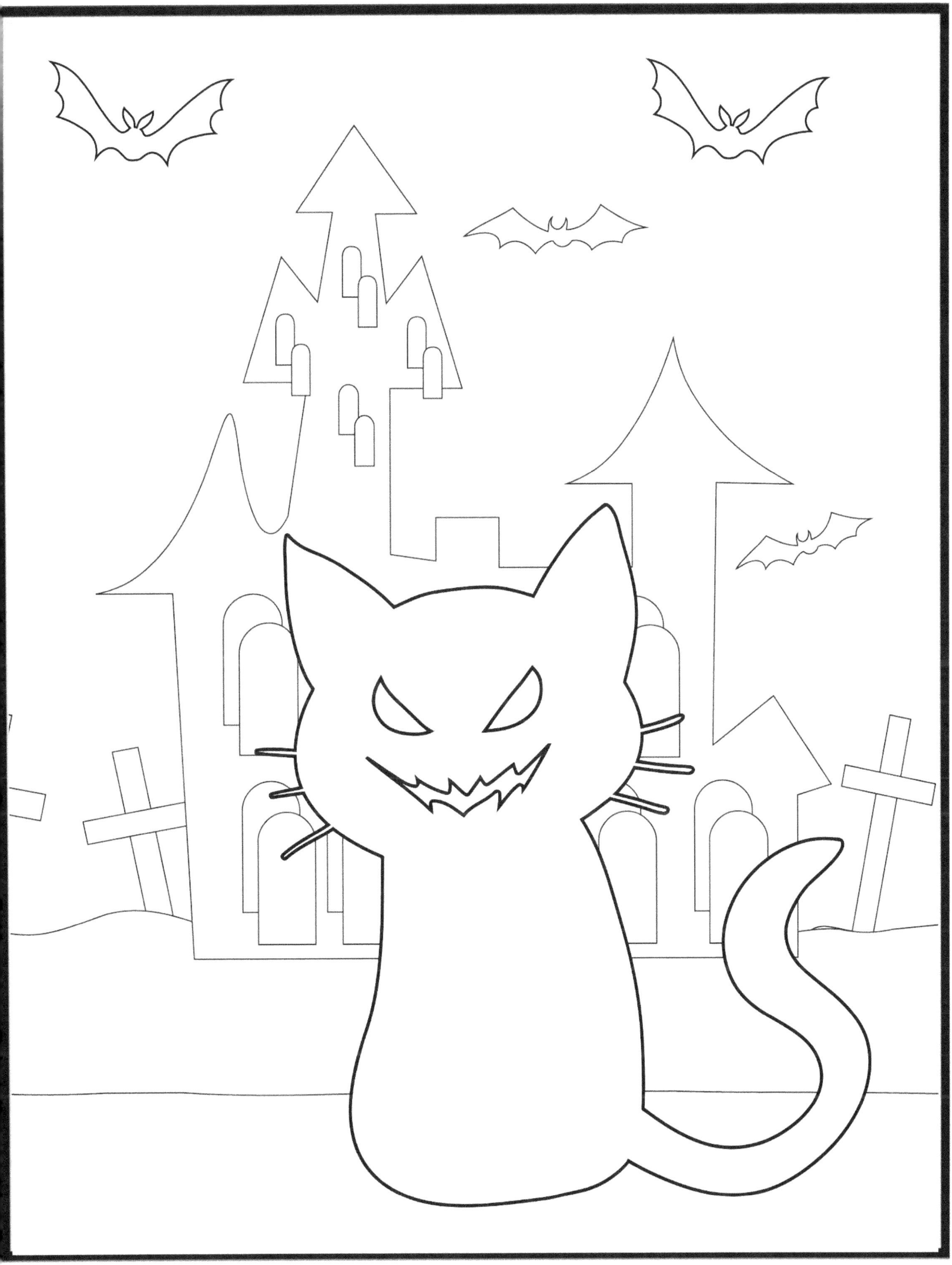

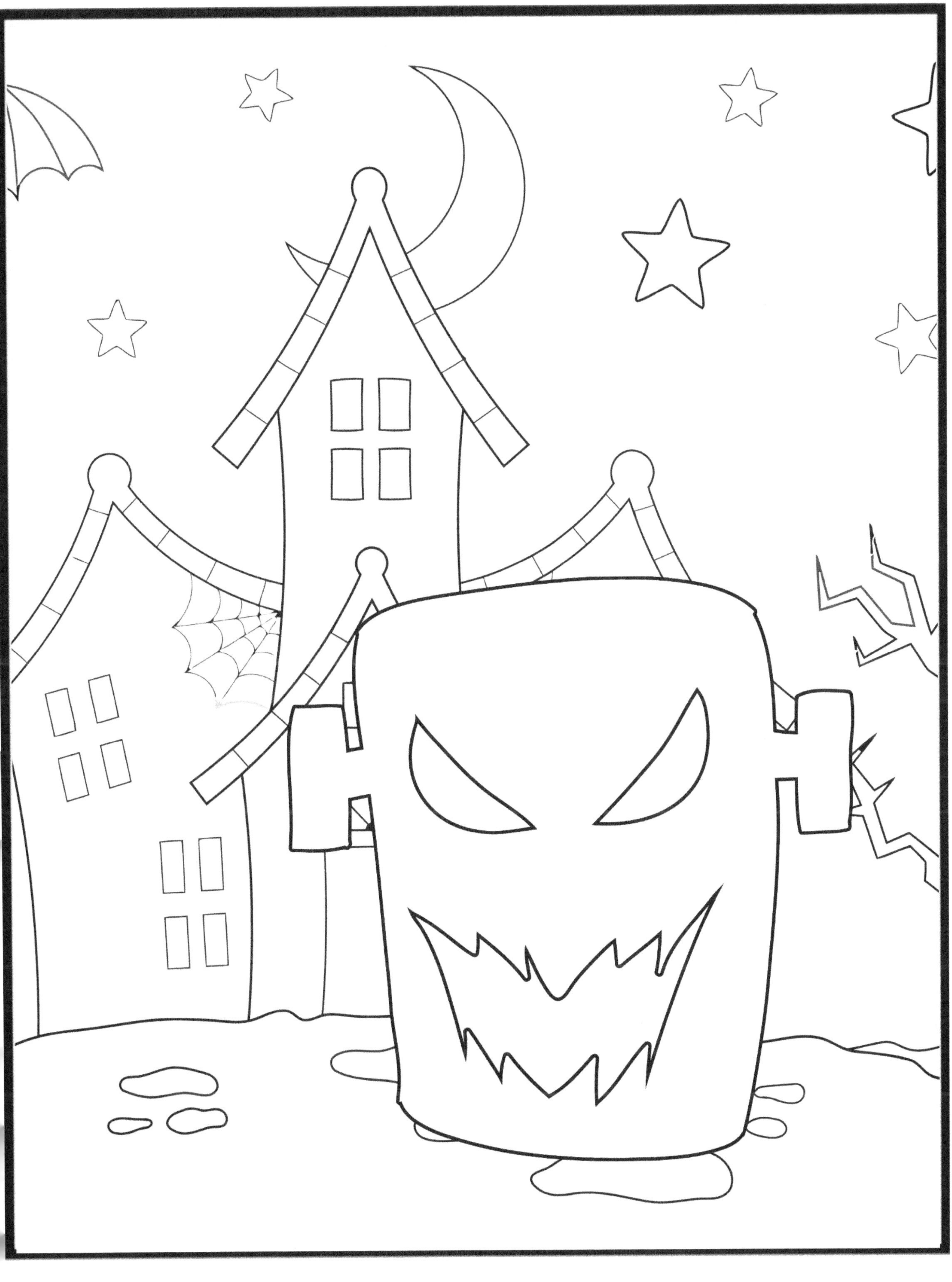

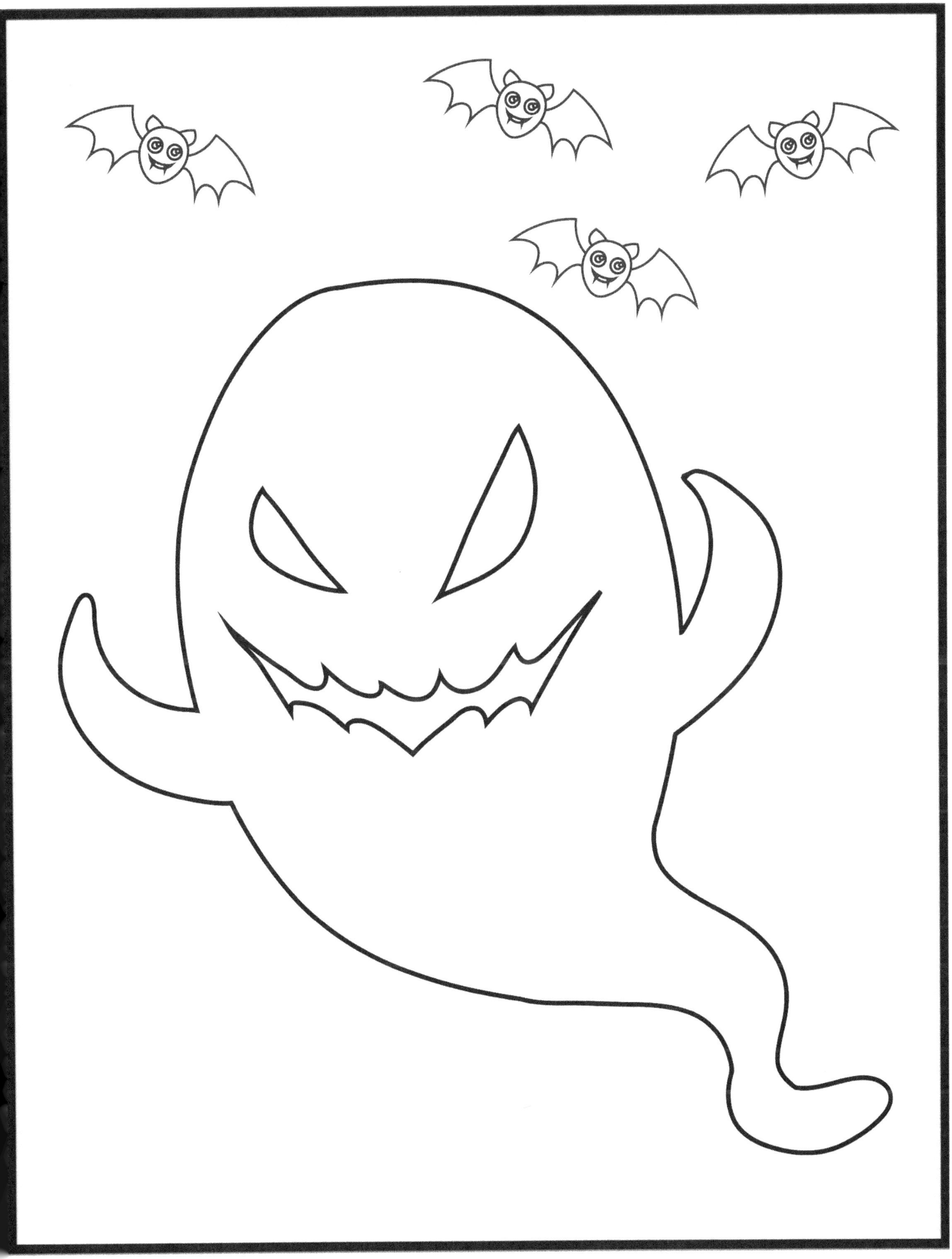

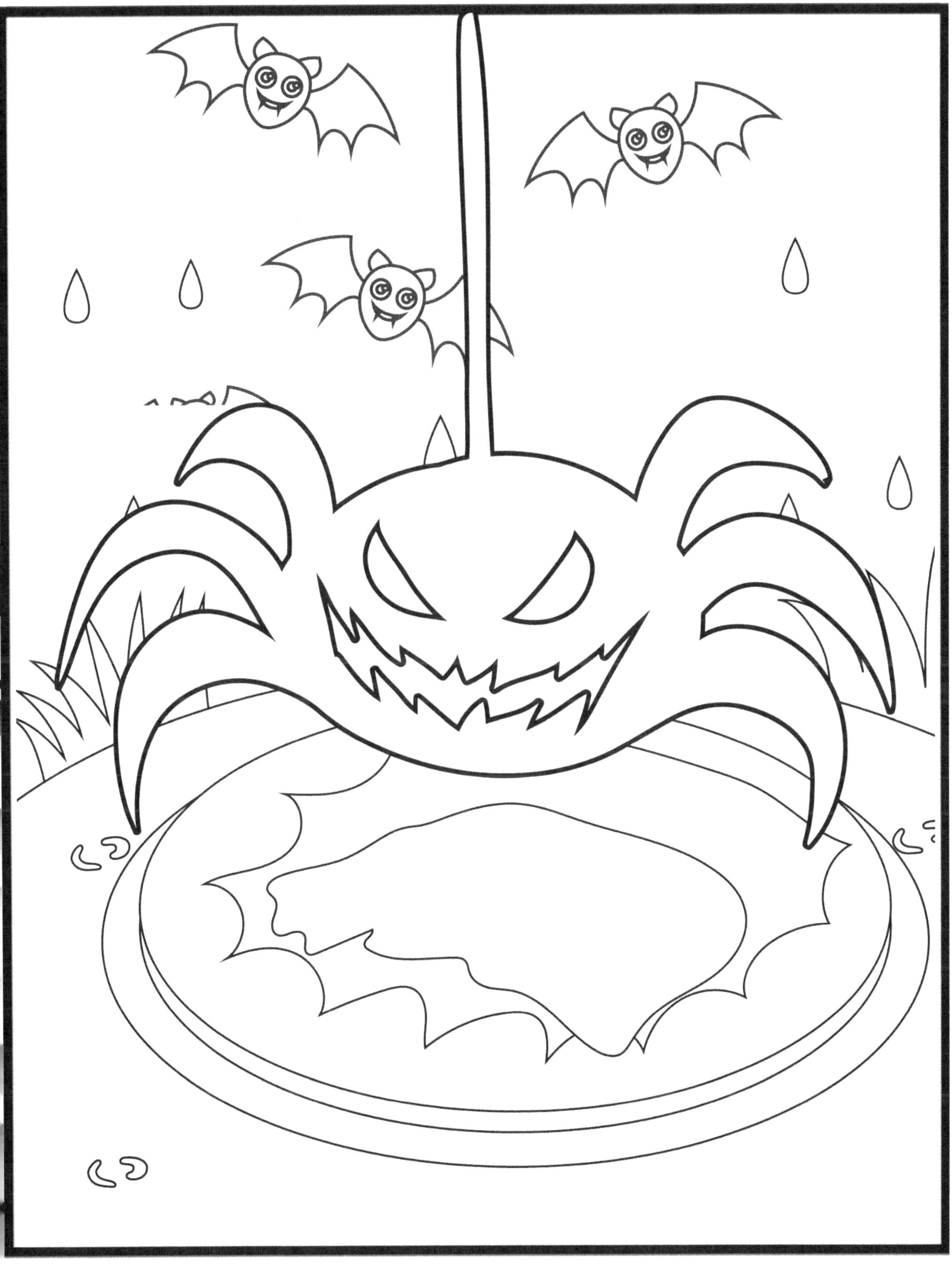

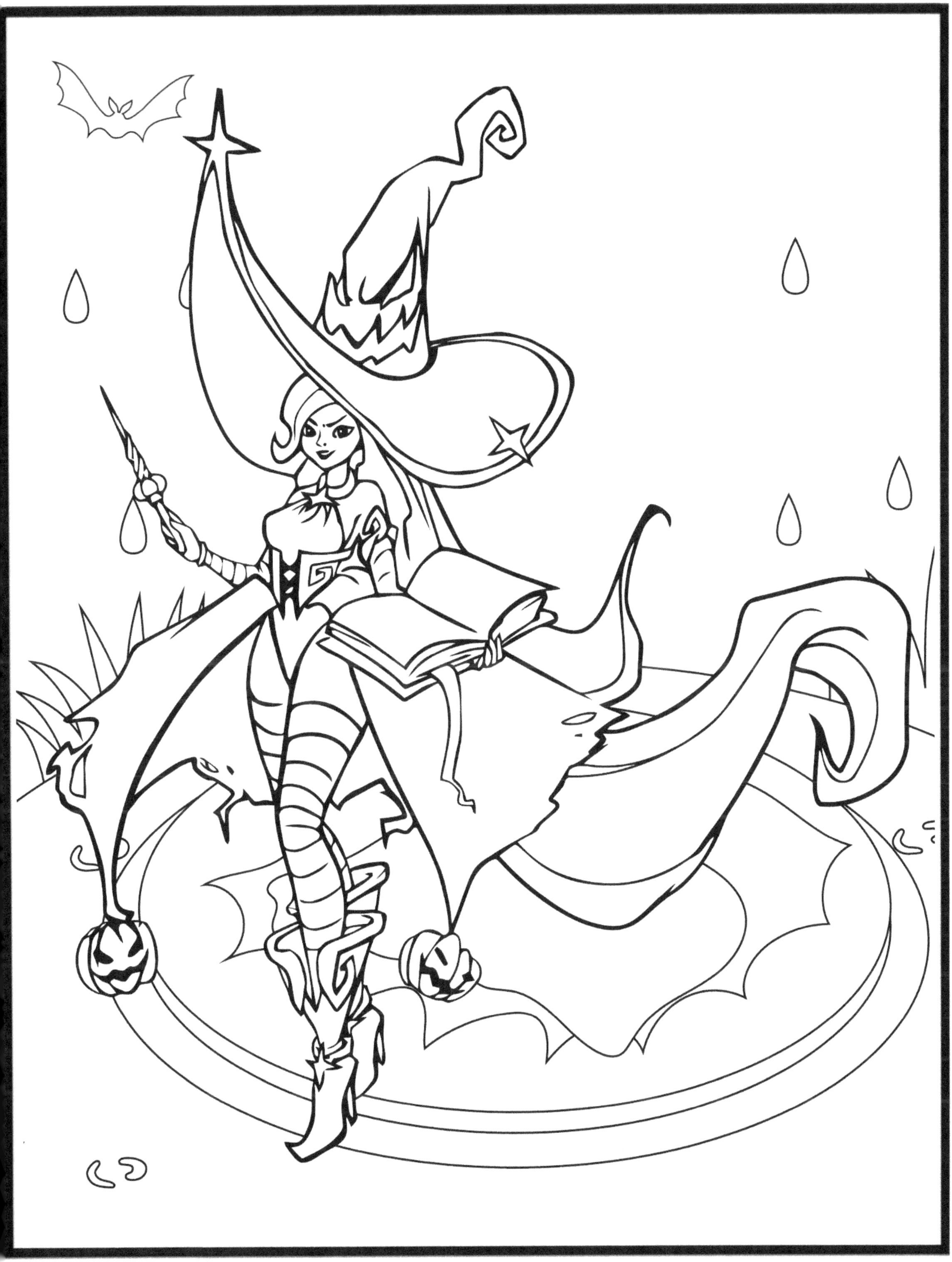

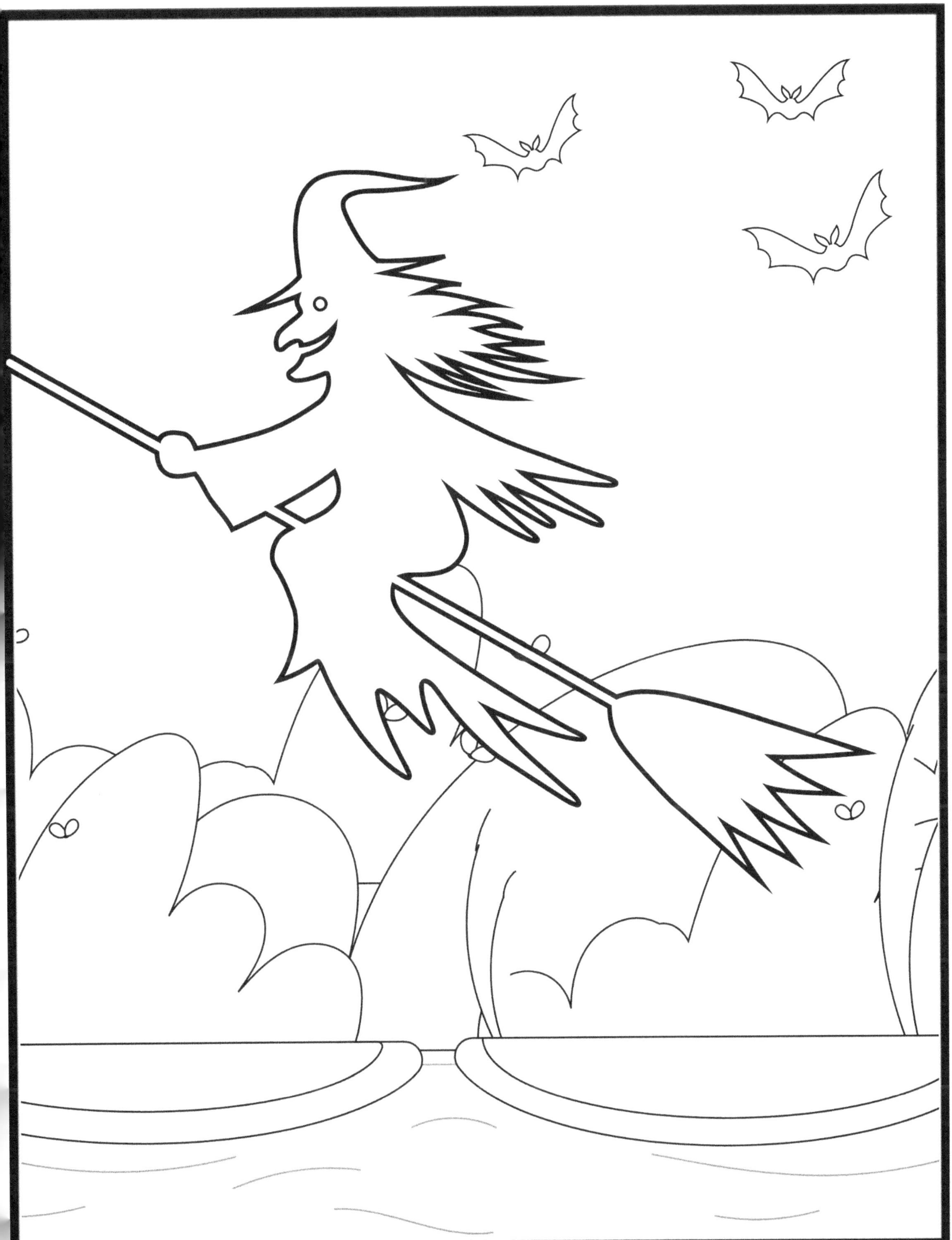

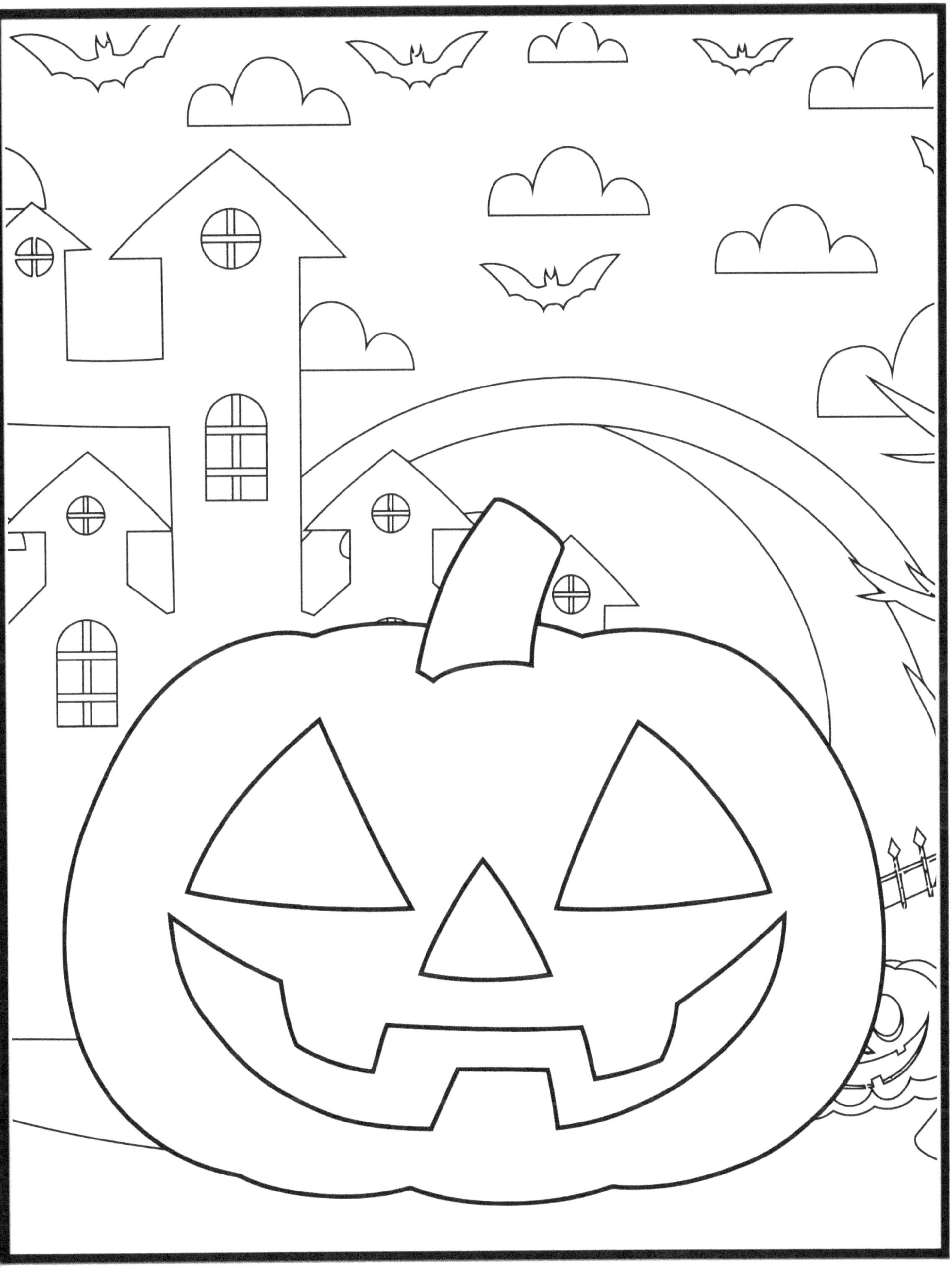

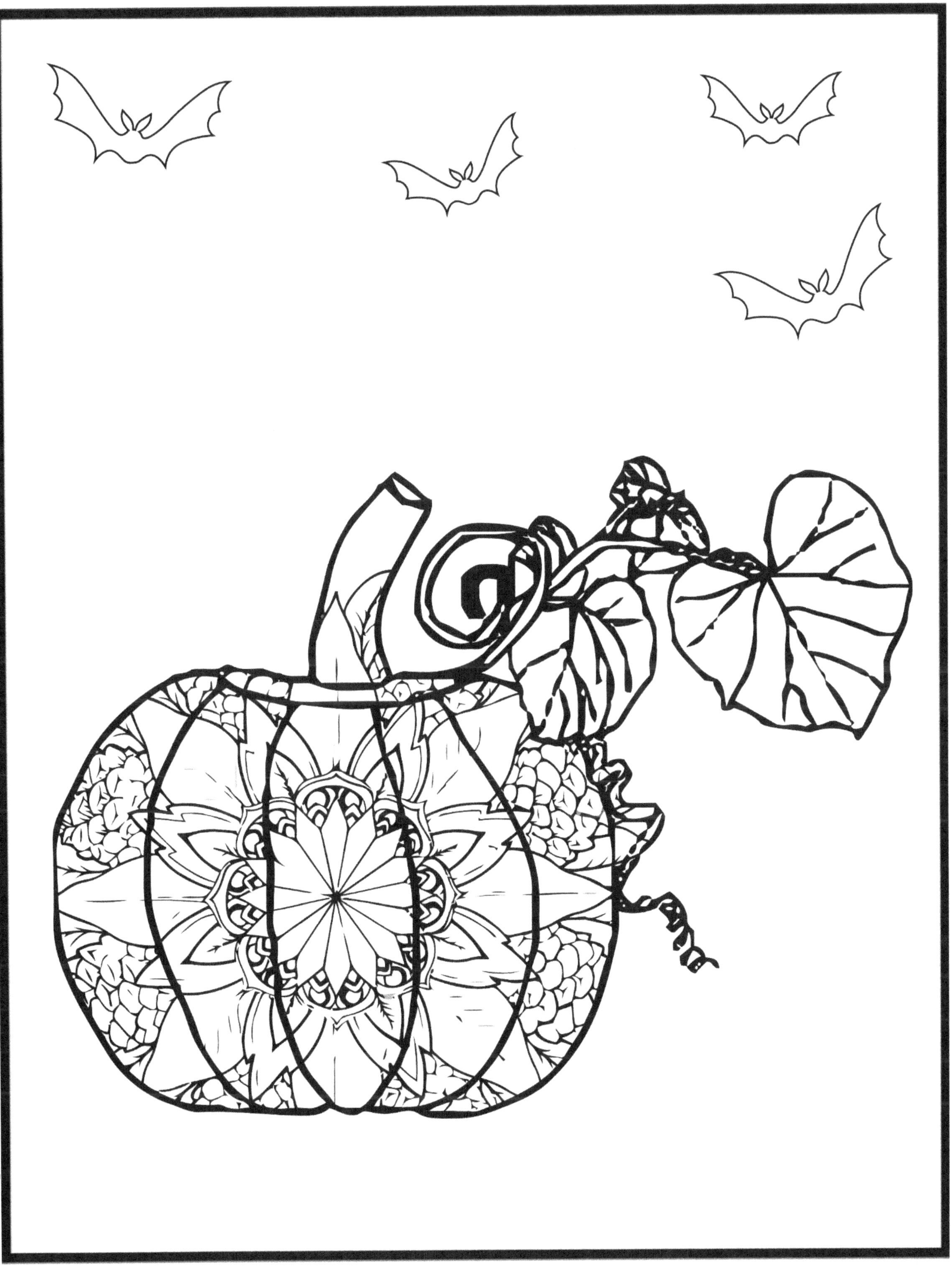

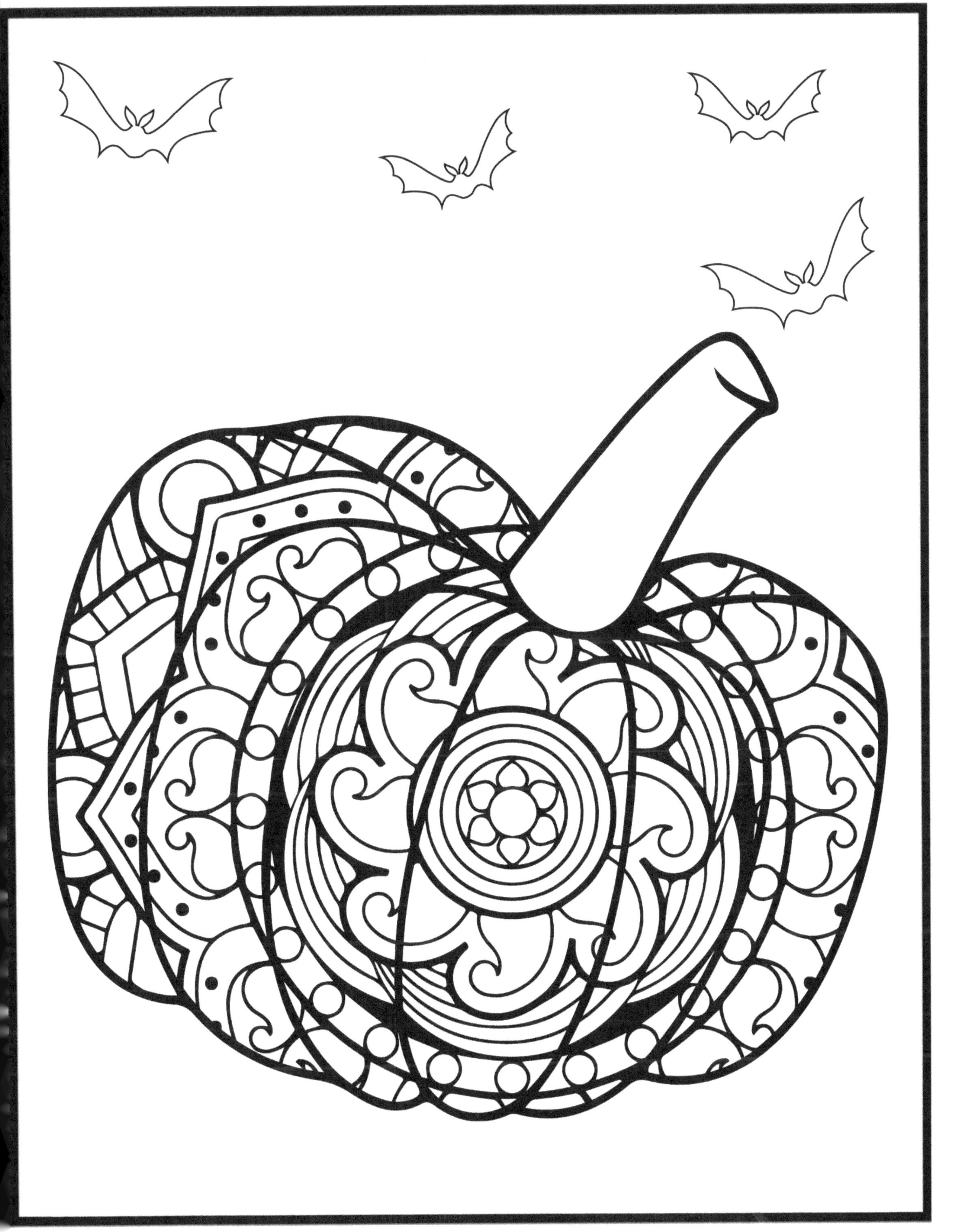

www.ingramcontent.com/pod-product-compliance
Lightning Source LLC
Chambersburg PA
CBHW060002230526
45472CB00008B/1910
9798454093808